Sing As We Go

SING AS WE GO

sing as we go

THE AUTOBIOGRAPHY OF

GRACIE FIELDS

DOUBLEDAY & COMPANY, INC., GARDEN CITY, NEW YORK
1961

The extracts from *Sally* on pp. 88–90 and from *There'll Always Be an England* on p. 158 are reproduced by kind permission of the copyright owners, Keith Prowse Music Publishing Co. Ltd. and Dash Music Co. Ltd. respectively.

ACKNOWLEDGMENT

Thank you, dear Joan Reeder—"Our Jo-Jo"—for being a wonderful sympathetic listener, as without you I am sure this book would never have been written.

GRACIE FIELDS.

ILLUSTRATIONS

Following page 48:

Tommy and me when I was a "half-timer"
Jenny and me
As Lady Weir in *S.O.S.*
Archie Pitt and me
You can see what I mean about Monty Banks' grin
In a Scottish shipyard in wartime
Receiving the Freedom of Rochdale in 1938
With our boys in the Pacific
My fifth Royal Command performance

Following page 168:

Gracie Fields
My South African welcome
A welcome in Newport, Mon.
The Strube cartoon published during my illness
A curtsy for the Queen
Me with President Harry Truman
A scene from one of my early films, *Sing As We Go*
With Victor McLaglen in *We're Going to be Rich*
Brother Tommy and me
Mr. and Mrs. Alperovici

SING AS WE GO

I

WHENEVER I've wanted to get something across in life I've usually sung it, ever since the day I was born, though in Rochdale they didn't call it singing for the first twelve months of my life. I bawled, every single day.

My mother was only nineteen when she had me, on the ninth of January, 1898, and she didn't get much encouragement from anyone.

"If I were thee," said one long-suffering neighbour above my squawls, "I'd smother yon child in my shawl. Happen we'd all get some sleep then."

Fred, my father, agreed: "Chuck her through the blasted window," he urged. "I've got my work to do in t'morning and I can't stand it."

But my mother had other ideas for me. She'd had them since she was ten when, as Sarah Jane Bamford, the orphan of a couple of flighty parents, she was being brought up by a very strict aunt who practically lived in church.

At ten Jenny, as she was called, was already working in a cotton mill from dawn till dusk. But, on the evenings she was supposed to go to Band of Hope, she'd found she could sneak into one of the two free seats that the Music Hall used to provide, called, for some reason, "Poet's Corner."

There she heard girls singing. Jenny could sing. She sang

11

louder than anybody in church when she went with her auntie, and she could sing louder, and better, than any of the girls she heard in the theatre. From then on she was stage-struck and she remained the most stage-struck woman I've ever met in my life. <u>Oh, how she _wanted_ to be an actress.</u>

At fourteen she left her auntie to live with two other girls from the mill. At <u>eighteen she married Fred Stansfield,</u> my father, because when she first saw him he was wearing long pointed shoes and a huge American Stetson hat and she thought he must be an actor.

In fact Fred was only a Rochdale lad who had gone to be a sailor, an engineer on a cargo boat that went to California where he had spent his few savings on a big brown ten-gallon hat.

Jenny followed Fred's hat down Rochdale's main street, Drake Street. Each time Fred stopped to admire himself in a shop window Jenny stopped and fixed her clog.

After they had done this a few times Jenny looked up from her clog to find the man with the big hat stood over her. "Tha' seems to be having a lot of bother wi' yon clog, lass!" he said pleasantly.

Jenny flew at him, scarlet, as soon as she heard his voice. "Why, you talk like a Rochdale lad! You're nothing but an ordinary fellow!"

"How can I be an ordinary fellow when I'm wearing a hat like this?" You never could rattle my dad.

Jenny must have seen the logic in this; anyway, she agreed to marry him.

Fred turned up at the church with a large cigar to match his hat. He wasn't too pleased when the verger took it off him: "Ah want that back when ah'm done in there," he warned.

All he worried about while he was getting wed was whether the verger was smoking his cigar: all Jenny worried about was that she still wasn't marrying an actor.

Fred got a job at Robinsons' engineering works, and Jenny made up her mind that her kids would be actors, *all* of them, no matter how many she had. I was the first, and she wasn't chucking me through any window.

The window in question was above my grandmother's fish and chip shop, and grandmother was known as "Chip Sarah." She was Fred's mother. Fred never knew his own father but as it happened he didn't need one, "Chip Sarah" would have made a man out of anybody.

Her own life had not been easy, and her first work was in a Rochdale coal pit, as a door-minder. "My job was to open and shut the door for the pretty little pit ponies," she used to tell me. It sounded a lovely job but one day I found out what it really was.

Throughout the pits there were heavy iron doors sealing off each shaft to stop "fire-damp" explosions from spreading. Youngsters had to stand by these doors and tug them open when the coal trucks came trundling through, pulled by stumbling pit ponies; then the doors had to be shut again as soon as the trucks had passed safely into the main shaft.

Such was Chip Sarah's first job—when she was a little girl of six! In the noise and dust of the pits she stood opening and shutting an iron door for twelve hours a day. When she grew older and went into service she thought she was in heaven.

By the time she was forty she had managed to save about fifteen pounds and that's when she came to her young daughter-in-law, Jenny, and said: "I've just bought a barber's shop."

"Aye?" said my mother calmly, and went on thumping

out her bread dough. Since few men in Rochdale then could afford to get a barber to cut their hair—they always had their wives do it—the barber had gone out of business.

Most people would have thought Chip Sarah daft to buy such a business with her few savings but Jenny, young as she was, already had a deep respect for her mother-in-law's capacity for hard work, and for her shrewdness. She knew she got up at half-past four every morning to see her lodgers off to work, one way in which she'd managed to earn a bit towards that fifteen pounds. Now, if she had bought a barber's shop she must have some good ideas for using it. Chip Sarah had.

When the barber sold out she bought the lease of his shop and all his stock of soaps, razors, strops, shaving mugs and hair oils, then she held an auction sale herself, and sold the lot. With the profit she opened the place up as a fish and chip shop.

She couldn't read or write but she could work. She had married a man called Jim Leighton who'd never done a day's work in his life, but he could write. He came in useful for keeping the accounts on the slate.

Sarah could never remember the names of her customers. If she had, Grandad Leighton, as we called him, could never have spelled them, but between them they worked out a system for keeping a check on the brass.

Sarah had her own nickname for everybody. She would call out: "Sloppy Clogs twopence"—this was a woman who always shuffled her way into the shop in clogs a size too big; another customer who always bought cigarettes was "Packet o' cigs," because the first time he came in the shop and spoke with a cigarette in his mouth she thought he'd said someone's sick and ordered Jim to "fetch a long mop; somebody's sick."

I remember "Five Bob-piece," "Ma Big Ears," "Cold Again Joe," and many others.

Chip Sarah made her steamy little shop on Molesworth Street prosper, and I remember her looking like a gaudy Queen Victoria—she loved bright colours as I do—and diving down the bosom of her frock where she always kept her purse, to give me and my sisters a ha'penny each.

We looked forward to those ha'pennies for there weren't many spare coppers in our family. By the time I was six I had two sisters, Betty and Edie, and Dad was only earning twenty-seven shillings a week at Robinsons, though he'd settled down all right there and never seemed to miss the sea. He'd married his pretty Jenny and got three kids. He was satisfied.

Young Jenny wasn't. She could still sing like an angel and she still longed for a life on the stage, not for herself any more, but for us. With only twenty-seven bob a week coming in and three kids to keep anyone with less determination than Jenny would have seen herself, and us, doomed to the factories and the back streets, but not Jenny.

"Tha' mun get a rise," she kept on at Fred. "We're not stopping like this, we're going 'oop in t'world, 'oop! Not down!" I heard my mumma say that all my life, right from the very beginning.

The road that led to the mill passed her front door, and another was at the back, every road went to the factories from our street, but Jenny paid no heed. We were "going 'oop" despite the mill chimneys which towered over all the housetops in Rochdale, and over the lives of its people.

I always remember how quiet the town was when the mills were working, there seemed to be nobody on the streets but very young children and old folks, with a few mothers carrying babies inside their thick black shawls. Shawls were worn over heads and shoulders as both hat and coat by the women, with hair-curlers under them, big as mouse-traps.

The quietness of the cobbled streets is a wonderful memory of my childhood. I love Rochdale and I've never seen it as anything but a beautiful place. Though people have described it as a huddled, damp, hard little town, it was never like that to me; it was home, and I belonged there.

There weren't many gardens in our part of Rochdale and all the streets looked alike with their row upon row of small terraced houses. Front doors were seldom latched and neighbours wandered in and out whenever they pleased. If you were sick they'd scrub your doorstep, wash your pots and put a stew on to simmer for you without a word. You might never discover who had done it and, if you did, they'd try to make it seem like an insult: "Eeh—that old shin-beef stew? It was either give it thee or give it t'cat!" You just helped each other. — hard, yet helpful environment

Money and work were scarce. Fred still hadn't got his very rise, and Jenny still had her eyes fixed on the future and British the stage. She'd get us there somehow.

She scrimped and saved her twopences and threepences in the old teapot on the mantelshelf, and went out charring to buy us decent clothes. She taught us to sing, the louder the better, and she tried to make us beautiful.

Every night with her strong, work-roughened fingers, she twisted our hair into tight curls with strips of rag. We had nice hair; mine was blonde, Edie's dark chestnut, and sister Betty's glowed red as fire. We slept three in one big bed, brown, red and yellow curlered Topsies in rising seniority from the wall.

Betty in those days matched her hair, she gleamed with red mischief and while I slept she would regularly unpick the rags from my hair. It made Jenny mad to find me with tangled rats-tails hanging down my neck in the morning and she would slap me while Betty danced about with glee in her nightie and put out her tongue. Many's the time I willed myself to stay awake, my hands clasped firmly over my rags to keep them in place and to fight off Betty's mischievous fingers.

Because Mother was determined that we three Stansfield sisters should always look as though we were practically on the stage we were often late for school, for she always insisted on doing our hair again at the door.

We used to wriggle and fidget, protesting: "We'll be late, we'll get t'strap." Mother never heeded; she didn't mind if we did get the strap but go to school with hair untidy we should not.

I was a terribly shy child and I could never bring myself to speak to the teacher at all or do anything to defend myself. If we were late I'd just go in with my hand held out for the strap—and get it. Betty would go in crying and never get it.

It was the same at home, I was used to taking the blame for Betty. If Mother got cross with her she would clutch at her chest and fall on the floor with dreadful moans. Then Mother always went pale and said: "Oh, God, I've killed our Betty!"

Mother was always taken in by her, but I must have been a rotten actress; I didn't know how to start this sort of thing, and I could never speak out. Anyway I was the eldest, so when anything went wrong it was always our Grace's fault. I got reared on clouts.

When I was seven Dad got a rise, one-and-a-tenner, and Mother promptly loaded the furniture on a hand-cart and we moved. This was the first stage of Mother's "going 'oop," we had three rooms instead of two.

I knew Rochdale pretty well by now, where some of the big houses were, and all of the pubs. I used to help my mother carry home the "left-overs" from the kitchens of the big houses where she went to work, and my dad took me on long walks, with a stop every few yards while he went in and had one on Sunday mornings. On these rounds I got to know and revel in Dad's salty sense of fun. *Dad = the humour?*

Once a man was boasting in one of the pubs about some big peas he had grown on his allotment. "Ah'll bet thee," said Dad, "ah've got bigger peas than thee next Sunday!" The bet was half-a-crown, very big money in those days. Next Sunday Dad turned up with some beautiful peas: the boastful gardener arrived empty-handed. "Tha' wins, Fred," he said gloomily, "ah've not a pea left in my garden, somebody's pinched t'lot!"

The strange thing was that on Dad's allotment there was nothing but a shed and a few chickens, the chickens being a handy excuse for the real purpose of the shed which Dad ran as a betting shop. He'd grown those winning peas overnight!

My mumma was different. On Mondays when I went with her to the big houses I noticed how she always tried to talk "well-off," and I was very impressed with this until she came a cropper. *?*

One Monday she was talking to the lady of the house about her great-grandmother who had once been cook to John Bright, the first Rochdale-born Member of Parliament. Mumma was very proud of her great-grandmother's association with the "toffs," and "upper ten," and ended primly: "But of course, she's dead at present!"

The lady began to laugh. "Have I said something wrong?" Mumma asked quickly, and the lady explained. Then I felt terrible and Jenny got mad and said crossly, "Ee, Grace, I am a damned fool! I should stop trying to talk well-off," pulled her shawl about her scarlet face and walked me home fast.

When Mother went to these big homes she always looked for any posh magazines to see what the latest fashions were; then, with the money she worked so hard for, she would go to Polly Pickles, the dressmaker in our street, and get dresses copied and made-up for us three sisters. We were going on the stage, we had to look different. Pride burned fiercely inside her and she loved to do the neighbours in the eye and go one better than them, and they knew it.

One Whit Sunday she had special dresses made for us. Out came the money from the teapot and off she went to Polly Pickles with the latest fashion books and three lengths of violet velveteen. Proudly we were fitted into these frocks for the Whit Sunday parade. When she'd tweaked and pulled and buttoned and hooked us into place, she lined us up in front of her and surveyed us with satisfaction.

"Wait there," she said, and went to the window and peeped through the curtains to see if it was time to send us out. What she saw made her livid.

Across the road the three little daughters of our neighbour, Mrs. Colclough, were setting out for the parade, all in violet velveteen frocks identical to ours.

Little Mrs. Colclough, who thought everything that Mother did was wonderful, had sent her three girls to Polly Pickles too.

Jenny's lips went tight, "Tak' 'em off, tak' 'em off!" she commanded, and began to rip the frocks off us. "You'll not wear these for Sunday, you'll wear 'em to school, and play in 'em on Saturdays! I'll show that Mrs. Colclough." Poor Polly Pickles went through it, too.

In this house we had a tiny murky cellar instead of the usual coal-hole, and Dad had rigged it up as a gymnasium for us with a couple of trapeze bars from which I spent a lot of time hanging upside down. I badly wanted to be an acrobat.

One day Mother sent Dad down to fix two screws in the walls, and to tie a rope between them. On this she hung a blanket with curtain-rings. "Now you can play theatres!" she said firmly, and we didn't argue with Mother. We played theatres.

We invited the neighbourhood children in for pins and buttons admission money; I sang to them, Betty did comedy, and our little sister Edie who was just a baby sat at the cellar door and guarded the saucer of pins and buttons.

But when May Day came along I soon found I could earn more than pins and buttons with my singing. It was a First of May custom in Lancashire for children to dance around maypoles which were decorated with coloured ribbons, blossoms and fancy paper, and to collect pennies from passers-by. Most of these maypoles were saved from one year to the next, and there was one for each street.

I was going to join our street group but Jenny said: "Nay, tha'll have thy own pole." She helped me decorate a broomstick and showed us how to dance around it. It was such a little pole compared with the others that the children of our street would have nothing to do with it so there were only my two small sisters with me, and my best friend at school, Ruby May Diamond Victoria Rylands who, as you might gather, had been born at the time of Queen Victoria's diamond jubilee.

There was a great bond between Ruby May and me, and especially we shared a love of brightly coloured ribbons, and this had caused us to have a very guilty secret.

One day we decided to follow a funeral we saw going down our street. All the people were strangers to us but we trailed them right to the cemetery, watched the coffin lowered into the grave, the earth piled on and then all the lovely wreaths put on top. When everybody had gone we stayed there, gazing at the beautiful coloured satin ribbons with which many of the flowers were tied. They were much better than the ones we had for our hair; it seemed such a waste to leave them there to get wet and muddy. Very carefully we undid the bows on two bunches of flowers, and re-tied them with our own limp faded hair ribbons. Then we put the funeral bows on our own hair and went home.

I told my mother that Ruby May Diamond Victoria Rylands' mother had given me my nice new ribbon, and she told her mother that she had got hers from my mother. We were very pleased with ourselves, but we had reckoned without our consciences.

That night I had dreadful dreams. A ghost kept rising up and following me about saying in a hollow, echoing voice: "You stole my ribbon! You stole my ribbon!"

The next day Ruby May Diamond Victoria Rylands told me she'd had nasty dreams too. We both wanted to go and put the ribbons back, but we daren't go near that cemetery again.

Still, the ribbons on our maypole had *not* come from the cemetery, and were gay and profuse enough, but we still felt we needed something to give our pole a bit more shine. Then I thought of little Eva, the richest girl I knew! She seemed rich to us anyway. Her parents seldom let her play with any of us rough neighbourhood children, and she usually looked lonely; I was sure she'd like to join our maypole.

I found Eva. "Can you go home and put on your best white silk dress and come out with our maypole?" I asked her eagerly. Poor little rich Eva was thrilled to be wanted. She sneaked into her house, put on her best dress, and sneaked out again. We let her hold the broomstick maypole; in her posh frock she made the whole party look classy. She was our May Queen.

We trailed off down Drake Street, a rather forlorn little bunch with our skinny maypole, and I led the singing. We got a couple of pennies in our box, but I knew where to get more . . . outside the pubs that Dad went to. I led our maypole outside every pub I knew, and that was just about every one in Rochdale, and the more pennies we got the louder I sang.

I sang all the songs Mumma had ever taught me, louder and LOUDER and LOUDER. By the time I was on to: "Oh! the old church bells are ringing" huge crowds were following us. For the first time in my small life I got some idea of what it was like to have an audience listening to me singing; I felt different, enchanted, it was a wonderful feeling.

I sang and sang, rattling my box in front of everybody, and the pennies rained in. At the end of that maypole day we had eight-and-tenpence each in pennies, and Jenny was really proud: if I could get five hundred and thirty pennies by singing with a broomstick maypole, what couldn't I get on the stage!

For a long time now she'd been going to see Mr. Grindrod every day. He was the man who shouted: "Tuppence, fourpence and sixpence this way!" outside the Rochdale Hippodrome.

"Owt you can find me to do in there?" Jenny had asked him, and now Mr. Grindrod had news for her. They wanted someone to scrub the stage.

Jenny was in her glory. She scrubbed the stage every Sunday and I went with her with my duster and brush, and helped. Every Sunday we were in wonderland, backstage of a real theatre among the ropes, daubed scenery, the bare-walled dressing-rooms which "the theatricals" used! But this wasn't good enough for Jenny, we had to see the theatricals, the actors and actresses.

Dad got another rise and off we moved again, and then again, each time to what Jenny called "a better neighbourhood," though all the streets were exactly alike. It was Baron Street this time, and right opposite a theatrical boarding house. Jenny made us all sing our heads off every morning in case one of the theatricals might hear.

Dad was getting fed-up. We moved house so often that his workmates were asking him: "Where'll tha' be living toneet, Fred?" Every time he got a sixpenny rise, that meant another house, at sixpence a week extra rent.

"If we listened to thee we'd stay in t'same place all our lives," Jenny retorted. "Listen, Fred. We're going 'oop!"

Dad's trials were far from over for Mum now had another idea of how to get into the theatre; she'd taken in actors' washing. After that Dad and all of us sat under the drips of the wet clothes each night and we never saw our fire for months and months.

The first I knew of this was when I came home from school trailing Betty and Edie. Dad was still at work, and Mother was in the kitchen with two big parcels. She looked guilty.

"What's in 'em, Mum?" I asked while Betty's mischievous fingers were already undoing the parcels and pulling out some vivid blue cloth—a man's shirt.

"That's not our dad's shirt!" I said. Mother snatched it, "Will you be quiet!" The walls were thin between us and our neighbours.

"But it's not me dad's shirt," I persisted. I knew by heart each of Dad's two shirts, one for wear and one for wash. Mother grasped my shoulders fiercely: "You mun never tell a soul, Grace, but I've taken in washing, theatricals' washing, from t'Hippodrome!"

as a way in

"Theatricals' washing!" I was thrilled, so were Betty and Edie. We rooted through the things and Mother didn't stop us. Frayed shirts, patched silk chemises belonging to the theatrical ladies and drenched in scent, be-ribboned and be-ruffled underskirts with layers of frills, garments we'd never seen the like of before. Theatricals' washing! We cooed over the gaudy things while Mother watched us with a burning, angry kind of affection.

"Tha'll have to help me with them, Grace," she said. "We'll have to wash them and hang them in t'kitchen where t'neighbours'll never see." Going out to work quietly was one thing in Jenny's eyes, but openly taking in washing was quite another.

After Dad had finished his tea I helped Mother with the actors' washing and we pegged it in the kitchen and all round the fireplace to dry. Next night I stayed up late again and helped her to iron it.

On Fridays and Saturdays came the reward. "C'mon, Grace," said Mumma, "we'll deliver t'laundry to t'Hippodrome." We packed it into two big newspaper parcels and went to the theatre.

"Keep your eyes about you, young Grace," Mother ordered. "Watch everything you can, that's the only way you'll learn."

We went in through the stage door, into the dressing-rooms, then into the wings, and we stood there watching the whole show. We did this every Monday when we went to fetch the washing, and every Friday and Saturday when we took it back. It could have all been returned on one night or the other, but Jenny thought an extra night wouldn't hurt anybody.

Afterwards she would cross-question me on all I'd seen and heard, and if I missed a thing that her sharp eyes had picked out I was for it: what the theatricals wore, how they looked, what they said, and, most of all, what songs they'd sung. This was easy for me to remember. I had a quick ear and so had Jenny. If a new song came along we'd both be singing it on the way home. "Now sing it like they sang it on t'stage," Jenny would order, and I'd mimic whatever I'd seen and heard.

I did my mimicry to some of my friends at school too, and they were very impressed when I showed them what I'd seen backstage at the Hippodrome. This did something towards making me feel better about being left out of all the school concerts in which Betty and Edie were always included. None of the teachers would ever let *me* sing in school. Whenever there was a singing class I was always told to stop because I was "much too loud." Mum's idea was to sing loud, as loud as possible, and I did.

I was very upset about this till my "loudness" brought me the chance Mumma had been longing for. None of the little houses in our street had indoor lavatories, they were all at the end of the backyards, and six neighbours each used to give me a halfpenny to scrub and clean them out every week, and while I was doing this I always sang at the top of my voice, as loud as I possibly could.

One day a woman came rushing out of one of the houses to find me and ask: "Was that you singing, dear?" I nodded. "Well! I'm going to give you a penny for that." She was a pretty woman and didn't talk with a Rochdale accent. She looked at me excitedly: "I've been listening to you," she said, "That's a wonderful voice. Where do you live?" I pointed to our house. "Come on, dear, let's go and see your mother!" and she caught hold of my hand.

Mumma was at the washtub when I burst in. "There's a lady wants to see you about me singing!"

"My name is Lily Turner and I'm on the stage . . ." the lady began. She didn't have to say any more, Mumma

25

was already drying her hands and filling the kettle to make some tea for her at once. An actress! In our kitchen at last!

Lily Turner was a music-hall singer from the Midlands and for a few weeks she was "resting" in the theatrical digs, off our street. "I heard your little girl's voice," she told Mumma, "and I think she should go in for the singing competition at the Hippodrome. I'll teach her the song, and I think she'd win if you'll let her try."

Let me! Lily didn't have to persuade Mumma. Hadn't she always told us to sing loudly outside the actors' boarding houses in case someone on the stage might hear? Well, now it had paid off, one of the "theatricals" had heard.

When Dad came home I chanted gleefully: "I'm going to win a prize in t'singing contest, Dad." "Nay, you're not," he said as he sat down to take off his boots, "you're not old enough, you'll get sent to prison. Kids under eleven can't sing in public any more."

"Since when?" asked Mumma sharply. "Since last week," said Dad, unperturbed. "It's a new rule. I didn't make it, lass, it's the law. It were in t'papers, they read it out in t'pub."

"H'm," said Mother, "we'll see!" and I went to bed contentedly. Though I was only seven I knew I should sing in the contest, there was no law that could stop Mother.

Next day she dressed me in a purple velvet blouse and skirt, and did my hair to make me look older. I was very tall for seven and could easily have passed for a twelve-year-old by the time Mother had finished with me. Then she took me across to Lily Turner who gave me the first and only singing lesson of my life. I've never had one since.

The song which Lily taught me for the competition was called "What makes me love you as I do," only when

I sang it, in my best Rochdale accent, it came out sounding like "Waat maks me luv you as ah do!"

Lily's face was a study as she heard me through, then she asked gently, "Can't you sound your aitches, dear?" I'd never heard of aitches, and I could *not* say "WHat" no matter how many times Lily tried to show me. In the end, she decided I must sing "Quat" instead of "Waat."

> *"Quat makes me love you as I do,*
> *There's other girls as nice as you,*
> *Quat makes me think you're so divine,*
> *Quat makes me long to call you mine."*

That was my first song from a stage and, in spite of all the "quatting," I tied for first place with two others older than myself, and won ten-and-sixpence.

This even impressed Dad and one night he came home with the news that the boss of a smoking concert who'd heard of my success would pay me ten bob to sing for them. Soon I began singing for charity concerts all over Rochdale and more often than not the fee was a tuppenny pie for each performance. They were nice pork pies for tuppence in those days and the family used to tease me to take an umbrella with me so that I could carry my pies inside it and bring them home to share with the family. (And I'm still suffering from indigestion!)

Meanwhile Mumma was busy cultivating Lily Turner, who was the best link she had yet found with the magical world of the theatre, and Jenny was determined not to let her go. She baked sugar cakes for Lily, did all her laundry, and quite soon Lily used to spend many afternoons sipping tea with Jenny in our kitchen, and talking about the stage.

Then one day Lily came in in great excitement. "Jenny! I'm going to leave the stage; I'm going to get married." She mentioned the name of a rich Rochdale stockbroker who had been courting her for some time, but nobody knew if he was serious.

Mumma greeted this news with a wintry little smile. "Well, I'm sure I *hope* you'll be very happy," she said. "If you *can* make him settle down to be a steady chap, then good luck to you, Lily."

"What do you mean?" Lily asked quickly. Mother shrugged; "Well, I just think you're very foolish. I'd never leave the stage if I were you. I mean, how can you be *sure* you're doing the right thing, and once you've got wed and got a family you're stuck. If it *isn't* the right thing you're caught, and you can never go back to the stage then. . . ." Mumma kept talking and talking.

Poor Lily had come in so radiant with her good news, but before she left our kitchen Mother had persuaded her to go back on the stage for another year at least—and to take me with her! Mother wasn't going to let Lily slip out of her hands into married bliss with me still not on the stage.

My first performance with Lily I remember was at Burnley, eighteen miles from Rochdale, and to get there in time we had to catch a train in the early afternoon. "What about her schooling?" asked Dad, and Mum told him, "You'll write a note to t'teacher and say she's sick."

"Ah'll not," said Fred firmly.

I was looking through the attendance register of my old school a year or two back when I was in Rochdale, and there it was, on nearly every page: "Absent. Sickness. Note from Father."

When we got to Burnley Lily didn't have me on the stage with her; she arranged that I should have a seat in the gallery and, when she had done her song, I was to stand up and sing the chorus back to her.

Mother didn't like this at all, it wasn't what she called

being "on the stage." Then one night when I stood up to sing an elderly woman sitting next to me sloshed me heartily with her umbrella and told me to "shut 'oop." She thought I was a little hooligan trying to spoil the performance.

This was Mother's big chance, and she made an outraged scene which was so effective that at the next theatre I was on the stage, with Lily, in a brown velvet dress with pink ribbons which had been made from one of Lily's old stage dresses.

There was a terrible argument over this dress afterwards; Mother wanted to keep it, the first dress "our Grace" ever wore on the stage, and Lily wanted to keep it too. And, since Lily had it in her lodgings, she did keep it.

"A'reet," said Mother grimly. She had just laundered Lily's wedding dress, so she kept that! They were both too stubborn to hand over to each other the dress they didn't want for the one they really wished to treasure.

By now Mother decided I had enough experience to go on the stage properly all the time, and she found that a juvenile troupe, Clara Coverdale's Boys and Girls, were in Rochdale. She went to see Clara Coverdale and returned triumphant. I was going to be one of the Girls and be a dancer on the stage.

On my first night away from Rochdale on tour in Hull, the kids in the troupe gathered round me. "How old did you say you were?" they asked. I answered innocently, "I'm ten."

They didn't like this. They were all fourteen to sixteen years old and adolescently wise; they resented a child of ten being put among them and they had their own solution to such a problem.

"Done much dancing?" they asked. I shook my head. "Can you do the splits? And a backbend? Can you pick up

29

a hanky from the floor behind you with your teeth?" I couldn't.

"Well, we'd better teach you," they said, and they did, on the bed where four of us were to sleep on my first night away from home.

They strained the ligaments of my legs and arms and bruised all my bones; my thighs, knees and ankles were puffed, inflamed and swollen; my neck was badly pulled. I had to hold my head between my hands before I could even swallow water, the pain was so bad.

I spent that night on the edge of the bed while three healthy girls snored soundly alongside me. I couldn't sleep at all, it was throbbing agony even to lie still. I just cried with pain all night. ✗ trauma

The next day I couldn't dance, nor the next, nor the next. I told Clara Coverdale I had the toothache. I was sick. I tried hard on the fourth and fifth days to move properly, but still I couldn't. At the end of the week I came home, hardly able to walk. I hadn't been on the stage once.

Father grunted: "Shove her in t'factory and put a stop to all this nonsense." It took all Mumma's determination to win me another chance, this time with a troupe called Haley's Garden of Girls, aged fourteen to eighteen. I was still only ten.

I did learn to dance and sing with this troupe but as soon as we were away from the theatre the others gave me all the errands to run. While I was carrying jugs of hot water to the bedroom I surprised one of the older girls with the son of the boarding-house. The girl grabbed me and said, "Here, give her a taste, I'll hold her!"

Somehow I scratched and fought myself free and ran in silent terror to my bedroom where I shoved a huge chest of drawers, that only my panic gave me the strength to move, in front of the door. I wouldn't let anybody in all night.

Next day I was too ill to know what was going on. Mrs. Haley had to break the door open and she found me gasping and twitching with St. Vitus's dance.

I had to spend six weeks in Rochdale Children's Convalescent Home at St. Anne's-on-Sea after that, and it so frightened Jenny that when I came home she sent me to school in Rochdale for a whole year.

what happened?

This was better than going to a different school in every theatre town but even so I wasn't very happy and this was because I was a "half-timer."

I'd been running errands for a bread and cake shop to earn a shilling a week and yet again Dad had said: "Shove her in t'factory." This time he'd won.

Most girls went into the mill when they were twelve; one week they worked there in the mornings and went to school in the afternoons, next week the other way round, hence the name "half-timers."

We used to get up at five A.M. for the mills when Old Amy, the knocker-up woman, came and rapped on our bedroom windows with her pole. Each family paid Old Amy tuppence a week to be awakened, and it was no use shouting "Righto! Amy," when you heard her tap-tap in the darkness, she just kept rapping till she saw your face at the window; then she knew you were out of bed and went on to her next customer. As Amy trudged down the street the candles and oil-lamps lit behind her in each little window, and in each house the kettle would go on for the tea. Outside you could hear the clogs of the early mill workers, the men who had to get there first to tend the furnace fires.

When the mill wanted the rest of us, half an hour later, it whistled. The buzzer we called it. "Quick, Grace, t'buzzer's gone." Five minutes afterwards the big gates were shut and if you were not inside you lost a day's work.

I was a cotton winder, but I can't ever remember doing much work as I was always three-quarters asleep when I got there at six and, by the time I'd come-to the girls would be saying a "C'mon, Grace, give us a song and we'll mind your frames." Into the din and clatter of the machinery I'd bellow out every song I knew while the others would keep a look-out for the boss and give me the signal to pretend I was working as soon as he appeared. Then in the afternoons I'd go to school, but I never learned much.

About this time, our next door neighbour, "Old Fred" we called him, came to live with us—just for one week—as he had grown too old to keep house and take care of himself. He said he was going to live with his sister or brother in another week's time, but we never saw either his sister or brother. We liked him and he liked us and he stayed with us till he died.

I used to sing to Old Fred and do imitations for him; his toothless chuckle used to encourage me. One evening he came in to tea with news that a Miss Jessie Merrylees, billed to appear at Rochdale New Hippodrome, was sick at her digs and the management was going crazy looking for a substitute performer.

Mother's nostrils flared like a war-horse, this was another chance, from heaven! On Monday night the substitute performer was: "Young Grace Stansfield, Rochdale's Own Girl Vocalist" in a dress hastily made by Polly Pickles, with star-shaped silver spangles on it. "Stars," said Mother. "Like you'll be one day."

That was a wonderful week and with thirty-five shillings paid to me at the end of it not even Dad could protest; he was earning thirty shillings. Old Fred's faded grey eyes glistened with pride, and the management kept me on an extra week.

This set Mumma working things out in her determined brain. If I went back to the mill after this there might never be a new miracle, never another chance. I should stay at home to look after my sisters Betty and Edie, my baby brother Tommy, Old Fred and Father. Mumma decided *she* would go to the mill.

She was still only thirty-two years old, slender with a waist I could nearly span with my childish hands. She was proud of her tiny waist and pulled in her corsets till she nearly choked; even all the hard work and worry had not been able to fade her youthful prettiness, and nothing could dampen her ambitions for the stage. When she told me what she was going to do, impulsively I moved to put an arm around her, sensing, child though I was, and used to seeing work, that already she had had her share. But, as always, she pushed me away with a kind of rough affection. "Nay," she'd say if you ever went to kiss her, "don't be soft."

Looking back I can't help feeling that hidden deep down there was a great yearning in her to be treated tenderly and cherished, but she would never let anyone be gentle with her or allow herself to be demonstrative. Once you gave in to feelings, you were done. She jabbed us all in the face with her fierce ambition and hurried on. We were "going 'oop!" and there was no time for softness.

So Jenny went back to the mill and I stayed at home till I was fourteen and May Day came round again. That week another troupe of juveniles were playing in Rochdale and I decided to take my maypole round to their digs, and sing outside the windows. They leaned out to listen, and when I'd done they clapped and their boss came to see Mumma.

It was arranged that I should join the troupe the following week at Blackpool.

Father was angry. "Off again on that nonsense!" he shouted, "I won't have it." The train fare to Blackpool was four and a penny; none of us had it and Dad refused to pay it.

He and Mum had such a row that we kids all ran out and I ran across the street to my friend Norah Tilison's auntie. "Me Mumma and Dadda are having such a row, and I can't get the money to go to join t'troupe in Blackpool," I sobbed. "Ee, luv," said Norah Tilison's auntie, "don't take on so, we'll find a way yet."

I ran back to our house again where the row was still going on, but Old Fred signalled to me. "Grace," he whispered, "ah've just read in t'paper there's a singing competition in Middleton tonight, wi' cash prizes. Do you think you could get there?"

Middleton was the next little town to Rochdale, but I didn't even have the bus fare. I ran back in more tears to Norah Tilison's auntie. "That's it!" she said. "I were just reading about it too. Now stop your scriking, young Grace, I'll treat you." We went together on the top of the tram.

The first prize was five shillings, and the judge awarded it to me, but there were shouts of protest from the audience: "She's not a Middleton girl!" The judge then awarded me the second prize, half-a-crown. "No! She's not a Middleton girl." He tried to give me the third prize, a shilling. Again he was shouted down.

I wanted to cry, I wanted to cry very badly, but I wasn't going to, not in front of all those Middleton foreigners! As we were leaving, the judge came after us. "Here," he said, "I'm sorry, my dear, you *should* have had the first prize, Middleton girl or not." And he handed me five bob out of his own pocket.

It was so late by the time we got back to Rochdale that Norah Tilison's auntie decided I'd better sleep that night with her rather than go home in all my excitement and start the row going all over again.

I *was* so excited that I couldn't sleep properly, and she, poor soul, suffered from asthma and woke up in the night to use a spray to help her to breathe. This so startled me that I leapt out of bed and started running all round the room which made her laugh, and that made her asthma worse. She often said afterwards that getting young Grace's fare to go away to the stage had nearly killed her!

But I *had* got the fare, and I went to Blackpool to join Charburn's Young Stars at four shillings a week, as Gracie Fields.

2

CHANGING my name from Grace Stansfield to Gracie Fields had been Mother's idea after she had been told by a theatrical manager that I could never become a star and have my name in big lights as Grace Stansfield—it was far too long a name and would have to be cut short. So Mother played around with the idea of Stana Fields, Anna Fields, but neither sounded right she said. Eventually she came up with "Gracie Fields," which everyone agreed would be easy to remember and would fit over the top of any theatre in big letters. And the day I lost my basket on Leeds Station made me quite sure that the change of name was not only a good idea but also a good omen.

When I had got a rise, of four shillings, I had saved like mad to buy something I'd always wanted, a real theatrical travelling basket for my clothes. It had four small wheels on the bottom so you could push it along, and my new initials, G.F., painted on it in big black letters. In the confusion of the station platform, my basket had been put with some other baggage, also labelled with the same initials, G.F. As I went forward to rescue it, I saw the owner of the other baggage was none other than the great George Formby senior, who was my favourite comedian and my

36

idol. I longed to ask him for his autograph but I couldn't pluck up enough courage. I was just contented that my initials were the same as his, and I thought it an honour and a good omen for the future.

But Jenny was not nearly so easily satisfied. She had made me send her the show's notices from each town and, as I'd been singled out for mention in every one and was still only getting eight shillings a week, that was not good enough for her. I was to come home and launch out on my own.

I'd been with Charburn's Young Stars for nearly two years, and I didn't want to leave them. Jenny insisted. We were still "going 'oop" but it didn't work out quite like that for a while.

I arrived back in Rochdale very pleased with myself, and with my theatrical basket. I pushed it all the way home from the station, hoping everyone would see.

The first thing Jenny made me do was to imitate for her, and for the neighbours, all the great stars of the music hall that I'd seen while I was on tour: Gertie Gitana, Maidie Scott, George Formby senior and Victoria Monks. Years afterwards, at a charity matinée, I was deeply moved when I saw Gertie Gitana imitating *me*, but then, while I was still fifteen, it didn't look as though I was ever going to get any work in the theatre again.

Jenny said I should have some professional cards printed, and we took the first one to the Rochdale theatre box office because, as a pro., I could get complimentary seats by showing my professional card.

The manager read it: "Gracie Fields, versatile comedian."

All we got out of him was: "How long have you been a man?"—and the way to spell "comédienne." Jenny was that mad she stalked home and threw all the cards on the fire.

Months went by and I was still out of work. My theatrical basket was shoved in the cellar. Dad and the neighbours began their usual chant: "Put her back in t'mill."

I was booked for one week at the Palace, Oldham. On the last night the proprietor, Mr. Ernest Dotteridge, asked me to sing a new song. I learnt it all right, but I forgot to tell the band I was doing it, or to give them the music.

I began my new song, they began the old one. Neither of us would give in. The louder they played the old one the louder I sang the new. In the middle of this chaos the stage manager dropped the curtain on me before either of us could reach the end.

I crawled back to Rochdale and spent all Sunday staring through the window of the little bedroom I shared with my sisters Betty and Edie. From there I could see the mill chimneys fairly beckoning to me.

The next day a letter came from Mr. Dotteridge: "We must not condemn a good week for one bad performance." He offered me a season with Cousin Freddy's Pierrot Concert Party at St. Anne's-on-Sea.

I didn't want to take this. When I'd been at St. Anne's-on-Sea in Rochdale Children's Convalescent Home with St. Vitus's dance I had told everybody I was going to be a big star performer. I didn't want them to see me as a pierrot! Also the pay was only three pounds a week, and I had set my heart on getting five pounds when I began on my own. "Three pounds is three pounds," said Mother firmly. "We need the money." So I went into Cousin Freddy's Pierrot Concert Party.

The comedian was Fred Hutchins who put in a sketch where I had to come on as a laundry girl who won't leave till she's been paid. In the crazy fashion of theatrical sketches he was supposed to have a magic wand that turned me to stone. "Make a fuss, raise your voice, say anything you like," he told me, "but when I touch you with my wand you must freeze in whatever position you happen to be. Understand?"

I nodded. At the first performance I barged on to the little stage in front of the rows of green deck-chairs carrying my laundry basket. I got so many laughs that Fred never touched me with the wand at all. We just kept on ad-libbing and the audience loved it.

Fred Hutchins taught me two things: how the generosity of a good performer leads him to "give" the stage to the one who is getting the laughs, and, how *not* to mind being laughed at! "Versatile Comedian" I may have called myself, but I hated being laughed at.

When I'd been with Charburn's Young Stars they'd given me a sentimental number called "Coax Me" to sing to one of the boys. I suppose, quite unconsciously, I'd clowned it. Anyway the audience roared with laughter and the management was very pleased. I wasn't. The first time they laughed I ran off in tears and refused to sing it again. People could laugh at my mimicry, I liked that. But laugh at me? Never. That hurt.

Fred Hutchins made me appreciate the enormous value of laughs and taught me a great deal about timing on a stage.

But there wasn't much to laugh about when I got back to Rochdale at the end of that season on the pier. I had weeks without a booking and then my dad had a very serious accident at work and had to go into hospital. There were no wages coming in and I had to earn some money somehow.

I got a small part in a pantomime and went off determined to make a success of it. The part wasn't much and

39

the only thing I liked about it was a good song they gave me to sing. The audience liked it too. On the First Night they clapped so long that it held up the show. But it only happened on that one night. After the curtain the girl playing the lead insisted it should be taken out.

That was my first experience of stage jealousy, and I hated it. I was miserable in the show, miserable in my digs, miserable about the way things were at home and sending every penny I could save back to Rochdale.

Mother sent Betty to be with me for Christmas Day and we had no money for anything special but I thought I could stretch as far as buying two oranges.

We spent ages looking at a fruit-shop, and bought the two biggest ones we could see.

We saved them up to eat as our Christmas treat when we got back to my digs. When we skinned them they looked funny, when we tasted them they were bitter and sour. "Ugh! Grace, I don't like them," said Betty, and the bitter sharp fruit seemed the last touch of misery on that Christmas; even the oranges had to be wrong. It took a long time for us to find out that what I'd bought had been grapefruit!

When I got back to Rochdale Dad was still in hospital and things were worse than ever. It was an achingly cold winter and we crouched around the kitchen fire where we were down to burning strips of box-wood. Old Fred the lodger began to cough.

I started going through the lists of theatrical agents and wrote to one in Nottingham. I took the only photograph I had of myself in dancing costume and sent it off, and I only asked for a job in the chorus, thinking if I couldn't go up—well then I'd go down. Anything was better than going back to the mill.

I waited a fortnight for the postman to bring me an

answer. When it came the envelope contained only my precious photograph, cracked right across the middle where they'd folded it to make it fit. On the bottom of the ruined picture was scrawled: "Hardly suitable."

All that day Mum and I avoided each other's eyes. At last I said: "Mumma, ah'll go back to the mill."

She thumped her iron hard on the table. "Nay," she said, "tha'll not! Ah'll go back again myself."

The weather was bad next day. Old Fred went out in it. He did not come in for his meal at mid-day. It was late afternoon before he returned, soaked to the skin, eyes bright with fever, and coughing badly.

We had to send him to hospital. In delirium he called every nurse "Our Grace." He died a few days later. When they went through his belongings they found an envelope addressed to Jenny. Inside it was his will. He had left her his insurance money—one hundred pounds—and in his shaky illiterate scrawl he had written: "Tha' nos best how to spend it."

She did indeed. After she had paid our family debts, she took me daily to Manchester to learn tap-dancing. In the troupes I'd only been taught ballet. We went to call on all the theatrical agents. One booked me for a week at Chesterfield and another, a Mr. Percy Hall, wrote asking me to see him.

Mum and I used up a complete pad of paper trying to write a suitable reply. In the end a lady trick cyclist who shared the dressing-room answered his letter. Jenny and I descended on Percy Hall's office in Manchester the following week, I dressed in a tight new costume and an enormous hat. I even carried a cane!

Mr. Percy Hall winced, passed his hand across his eyes as though at a strong light and said: "For God's sake, girl, take off that dreadful hat!"

But he offered me six weeks' immediate engagements at five pounds a week. At last—five pounds!

"We'll make a little agreement," he said, signing the contract. It was an agreement for *ten* years. I was to get no less than five pounds a week, but, when I earned more, it was to be equally divided between Gracie Fields and Mr. Percy Hall.

Mum and I had been told about such contracts, but we were desperate. We signed.

We did not dream, nor did Mr. Hall, that in ten years the gawky girl in the silly hat would have played 4,000 unbroken performances of *Mr. Tower of London*, and would go on to play two London theatres at once, one at £100 a week, another at £200, *and* a night club at £300.

Still, it was 1915 then, and five pounds a week was the goal I had set myself as a solo act.

Mr. Hall booked me for six weeks, around Manchester, and then found me a part in a new revue to be called *Yes I Think So*. I met the cast in his office. One of them was a pale-faced young man who was to be the principal comedian. His name was Archie Pitt.

At that day's rehearsals I watched him and didn't think him very funny. He sang a song "Does This Shop Stock Shot Socks With Spots" that made me smile a bit, but the rest of his act seemed like rubbish. My favourite comic in those days was of course George Formby senior, and Archie Pitt was no Formby; he was a London Cockney comic. Lancashire folks don't often go for Cockney humour.

When I sang my couple of songs I noticed he watched me keenly, far more keenly, it seemed to me, than the owner of the revue who was paying my wages. When I'd finished he came over and said: "I'm not sure, but I think, I only *think*, mind you, that you may have something."

I stared at him and tried to walk away with dignity. I didn't like him much, he disturbed and unsettled me. His eyes were too constantly upon me, too penetrating. I tried to avoid him, but that wasn't easy. You couldn't avoid or snub Archie.

Mother had found me free digs in Manchester with a friend-of-a-friend of hers. When I'd gone off she'd said: "Remember, Grace, offer to help with the washing-up and make your own bed; only sluts come downstairs without making their beds."

I washed up. I made my own bed. I practically scrubbed out the entire house. It was miles away in a Manchester back street over a little grocery store and it was pretty dirty.

I'd been told not to waste my money on tram fares, so that I had to walk nearly three miles to the rehearsal rooms, rehearse for six and eight hours at a stretch, and walk home again. This, on top of all the housework I'd done, left me pretty well exhausted. Archie Pitt noticed my tiredness and soon found out the reason for it. When we left Manchester for Preston he insisted that I stay in the same theatrical digs as he did and instructed, with a curious insistence that was to pattern his attitude towards me for many years to come: "Remember, no housework."

I knew he was right, but I was ashamed to tell him I had done this in return for my free digs. However, although I went into his digs, I didn't want to see too much of Archie. I didn't feel at ease with him. I had my own combined bed-sitting room upstairs, but after the landlady had brought up a tray a couple of times she panted: "Dearie, these stairs! They're killing me. Now why don't you have your meals downstairs with that nice gentleman, Mr. Pitt?"

"I . . . I'll fetch my own," I stammered.

"Not in this house you won't, my little luv," said the landlady. "If you've got to have 'em up here, then you must, I s'pose." Her voice was not unfriendly but as she bumped down the many stairs to her kitchen, I felt very miserable. It didn't seem fair to give her all that extra work. I went downstairs to eat.

"Well!" said Archie, giving me the same keen look as I went in. "Nice to see you. Make yourself at home, Grace." But I couldn't. He made me feel uneasy, and I decided I didn't like him at all.

Yet in the theatre, when he went on, I waited in apprehension, worrying for him. I was sure the audience would never take to his jokes. I can still remember my amazement when he began to get the laughs.

He came off grinning, damp with sweat. And though I'd never ventured any opinion on his work he showed his quick perception in knowing what people thought of him when he said: "That surprised you, didn't it? Now let's see what *you* can do," and, as I brushed past him to go on for my songs he added quietly: "Good luck." He was still in the wings, smiling his approval, when I came off to roars of applause.

Archie watched me every night like that and, on my sixteenth birthday, that same week, he insisted on giving a little party at the digs for me and some of the company, and he bought a bottle of champagne.

Mum had always told us that the polite thing to drink was port and lemon, and that was the first time I'd ever tasted champagne. It made me dizzy enough to pluck up courage to ask everyone there for an autograph, and Archie scribbled in my book: "To Gracie Fields; one day you are going to be a big star."

We were on the road with *Yes I Think So* for eighteen

months. During that time whenever anything went wrong for me Archie insisted on putting it right.

I was a singer. The owner of the show was a singer too, and each time I made a success of a number he took it away from me and gave me another song to work up. But his apparently professional jealousy provided me with invaluable experience. Week after week I learned how to make a mediocre song into a good one by introducing different vocal tricks.

classic

When that tour ended my agent, Percy Hall, wired me to join another revue.

"You don't want to go to that," said Archie.

"Got to," I said. "It's six pounds a week, and anyway, I've got a contract."

"Do you want to go on being pushed around by agents all your life?"

"There's nothing else to do."

"Yes, there is. I'm writing a revue of my own, and I'm putting it on the road. Mona Frewer's going to have the lead and you can come as second leading lady, instead of the third, as you are now. We can all start out together."

"What about my contract? It's for ten years, and a half of everything I get over five pounds has to go to Mr. Hall."

"I'll deal with Mr. Hall," said Archie.

"Me mum'll want to know how much you'll pay me," I said, suspiciously.

"I'll talk to your mum," said Archie.

He had no money and knew he would have to spend the whole company's first week's salary on buying the props and the scenery, yet he settled with Mr. Hall and won Jenny over.

She saw more in him than I did, his native shrewdness, his drive, his love of the theatre and, above all, his determined insistence that I had "star quality."

Before we could open with the new revue Archie had written called *It's a Bargain*, he had to borrow forty pounds to pay the company's rail fares. That wasn't enough to pay for our lodgings as well, and we had no wages; they had gone on the props. Archie and I managed to persuade landladies to let us owe them a week's board, and Mona Frewer pawned her few jewels to help raise the funds.

Archie's three brothers, Edgar, Pat and Bert, were doing a comedy act in this revue. They called themselves "The Three Aza Brothers." This was brother Bert's idea. "Aza" was the trade name of a brand of cloth, and Bert persuaded the manufacturers to give them each a sample suit to wear on the stage in return for the advertisement. They were not distinguished comedians.

Mum came to see the show. There was a brick missing in the wall between my little dressing-room and the Aza boys' next door.

"Somebody should tell them lads they're no good," said Jenny contemptuously.

"Shhh! Mum, they'll hear!"

"Ah doan't care if they do hear," she said, indignantly. "It's the rottenest act ah've ever seen and they *ought* to hear."

They did hear. Bert agreed with Mum; he dropped out of the act and became our manager. He was brilliant at that. He may not have been much of a comedian but what he didn't know about managing a revue he soon learned.

He and Archie kept *It's a Bargain* alive for two-and-a-half years. During that time Mona Frewer's health suffered and she was often unwell. When this happened I went on for her as leading lady as well as doing my own work as second lead. Each performance lasted one hundred and ten minutes and there were two shows a night. Often I was on stage for an hour and twenty minutes in both.

46

Mother sent my sister Betty out to Archie as soon as she was old enough. Full of life, sparkling and fiery as her red hair, Betty wasn't too keen about being on the stage, though she was beautiful and had a good singing voice.

If ever there was a party in the digs, Betty was the star, but on the stage she didn't try too hard. However, with Betty, as with me, Archie scented talent, and he started to drive her.

I remember in one sketch she was supposed to be a passenger in a bus. She had no lines to say, so she just sat there, night after night, doing nothing except fall asleep. Then, right in front of the audience, Archie suddenly turned on her and hissed: "If you can't do something original, bloody well stay off!"

Next night she stopped the show.

She was only fifteen but that was the effect Archie had on you. I knew it well enough.

Meanwhile brother Bert was managing us with fanatical zeal. He would go to the chiefs of big theatre combines and say: "I know you think we're not good enough for your better theatres but give us one week in the worst and we'll take it, on a percentage of the profits."

This worked. Bert would rove up and down the aisles with his notebook shamelessly counting the audience. He would be back in the box office before the house manager and stand by, with unwinking gaze, as the receipts were checked. Once he was thrown downstairs and an ink bottle flung after him after he'd said doggedly, and for the fifth time: "It's no use telling me you only took seventeen pounds, fourteen shillings, I _know_ you took eighteen pounds, three shillings and ninepence."

Occasionally, at the end of the week, Bert went ahead to the next town to borrow our fares from the theatre manager there, so that we could travel. He arrived Friday,

wired the money Saturday, we travelled Sunday. Bert cal-
culated that by Friday it was too late for the theatre manager to get anyone else so he'd *have* to advance us the
money.

Archie didn't care how we managed so long as we were
working. He shared my mother's conviction that we were
"going 'oop."

He'd been a shop assistant, commercial traveller, had
begun to do comic turns in pubs, then working-men's clubs.
Like many men from obscure beginnings who get on in
the world, Archie took no heed for today, he worked for
tomorrow. He'd seen in me the glimmer of something. I
was nearly eighteen now, and I was his. In two years he'd
got me hypnotised.

Archie had found in me a talent that might become big
and he stripped away the other acts without mercy to give
it room to grow.

Mona Frewer, graceful and delicate, who had started as
the star and who was being crowded off the stage by the
strident, loud-voiced girl I must have been, flared up one
night.

At that time mimicry was my star turn and Archie had
cut one of her favourite numbers to let me imitate Charlie
Chaplin. I'd nearly broken my neck trying to get his walk
right. Now I'd got it and the result was good.

Mona watched, laughed, and agreed it was good, but for
her it was also the last straw. When I came off she stormed
at me: "Imitations! Any monkey can do imitations! D'you
know what I think? I think it shows you've got no orig-
inality; it's just stealing other people's brains and material
because you can't think of any for yourself!"

Soon afterwards she left the show. She had fought as
hard as any of us for its success, I understood how she felt,
I liked her, and I am in her debt. Her words so shocked me

This is when I was a "half timer" I didn't look like this at work, but Mumma always saved up to have our pictures taken, and Tommy and I, the eldest and the youngest, are wearing our Sunday best

Jenny and me, when the hard days were just beginning to be behind us

As Lady Weir in S O S, the Sir Gerald du Maurier play, in 1928 See! No tammy and no kilt, I'm a lady now!

(Photo London Electrotype Agency Ltd)

Archie Pitt and me, at the beginning of his impresario days in the West End

You can see now what I mean about Monty Banks' cheerful grin and those merry, humorous eyes (Photo Dorothy Wilding)

Wartime—the Scottish shipyards—and as
grand an audience as anyone could know
(Photo Keystone)

(BELOW) Receiving the Freedom of my native
city, Rochdale, with Ald Bryning (LEFT) and
Ald Crowder, the Mayor, in 1938 I may have
been waving my hat, but I was shaking with
nervousness If you look at the picture at the
left you'll see why All the same it was the
proudest day of my life

Still wartime—in the Pacific now Wherever I went I found our boys always smiling, bless 'em.

My fifth Royal Command performance at the London Palladium, 1950
(Fox Photo)

that night that I've never done another imitation on the stage. She helped me to start finding something of what Gracie Fields had to give. Annie Lipman made me find the rest.

Annie, small, dark and determined, was a singer. She asked Archie for a job and was turned down. She asked Bert for one, and got it. Soon she became our musical conductor.

One night I was singing a number, a song I'd sung fifty times already, and I was bored with it. Annie looked as bored as I felt.

I was a bit tired of watching Annie, her face drooping with boredom, waving her baton in flawless rhythm. She looked like a sleepwalker. I decided to wake her up.

I started to clown the song with a burst of vocal acrobatics. Annie nearly dropped her stick. The audience howled. That's how I stumbled on the art of burlesquing a song and, in a way, I suppose, found myself.

In those two years Archie had found himself too. He'd made his own little theatrical company. He wrote for it, directed it, kept it going. He was impresario of his own little flock, his word their law, and we all called him Papa Pitt. He liked that.

He wrote another revue to keep us all together and called it *Mr. Tower of London*. It was a poor show and he knew it. "Never mind," he said, "we'll all work on it."

We all worked on it for a year and Jenny sent gentle Edie, my second sister, out to join us.

There was only the "baby," young Tommy, left at home now, and Fred, my dad, had been offered a job with a new firm that was going to London. Mum and he had lived in Rochdale all their lives. The offer worried Dad.

"Ee, ah doan't know about it," he said.

49

"Ah do," answered Jenny promptly. "The kids are working more London way than up North."

They went to live in Islington. From there Jenny sent young Tommy to join us when he was thirteen.

Tommy shared our circus of a life, travelling from theatre to theatre all over the country, and started doing his bit by selling picture postcards of me at each performance. He thought nothing of tramping among the audience selling my pictures while I was on the stage. Sometimes he made such a blooming row, clinking his change and stepping on people's feet, I could have sloshed him. I'll never forget one night when he was standing in the centre of the stalls behind Annie, our conductress. I was singing my most dramatic love song "As Long As He Loves Me"—when I heard, clonk, clonk, clonk—eleven pennies change, he told me later. A man had bought a photograph for a penny. He knew just what he had done, but like a young lad with the devil in him, he dared me to keep serious during the song. Tommy was always my best audience in comedy sketches.

Mr. Tower of London was in its fourth year of touring. In its fifth year I married Archie Pitt. Archie insisted.

I am easily dominated and Archie dominated me. For nine years, since I was sixteen, Archie had drilled me, encouraged me, driven me, helped me, and filled my life with work, work and still more work.

There had been nine years of touring with him. Nine years of travelling from one cold damp little theatre to another; no heating, no hot water, sometimes no theatre even, just a hall for which we had to hire a piano. Bad food, often bad digs, and two, sometimes three shows a day, and then Archie would keep me up till one and two in the morning helping him think up new ideas for sketches.

When I'm tired I get ridiculous, and when I'm ridiculous evidently I'm funny. Archie spotted this early, and he'd keep me tired and keep me up, ad-libbing and improvising lines with him until he'd got the sketch sufficiently polished to put into the show.

For weeks we toured the little mining towns in South Wales, and at the first one I was so tired when I went on to give a nine A.M. show to miners straight off the night shift, that I'd forgotten where we were.

I saw rows of sooty faces turned up to me, their smiles gleaming white in contrast when they laughed, and I staggered off into the wings and said to Archie: "How ever did you manage to get so many chimney sweeps at this hour of the morning?"

But by working this way "Mr. Tower" started to make money. In the provinces it gradually did good business.

I met no one except our little company. I went nowhere except in the trains on Sundays to the next theatre.

Gracie Fields, versatile comédienne, was learning fast, but Grace Stansfield, the kid from Rochdale, wasn't growing up at all. I knew nothing about any world outside the one Archie had built for me.

He'd taken over where Mum had—I was about to say left off—but she never left off. But when Mum wasn't with me, Archie was. He was not Svengali, but he was a passable imitation.

"You've got a big future," he said. "You mustn't wreck it by getting a husband who will distract you from your work."

"I don't want a husband."

"Yes, you do. You need a husband, otherwise you'll marry the wrong type before you know what you've done."

"I won't. I've never seen anyone I'd like to marry yet. I never want to get married."

"Marry me then," said Archie, "and life will be just the same as it is now!"

We had that conversation endlessly. I got tired first. I said "Yes."

"What are you going to wear for the wedding?" asked Betty, who'd already been a bride and married Roy Parry, the scenic artist with the show.

"Ah've got that nice new black dress," I said.

"You can't wear that," said Mum. "You *can't* wear *black* for a wedding." But I didn't much care what I wore.

The ceremony was at a register office in Clapham. I was twenty-five and Archie was forty-three. We hadn't much in common except the show. —she wears black ?

We went to Paris of all places for a honeymoon. We couldn't get a cup of tea, we couldn't understand a word anyone said, and we didn't know what to say to each other. The best bit of conversation we had was when he suggested we should go home and get on with the show. Then we felt at home, with ourselves and with each other.

Mr. Tower of London went on and on. At the end of six and a half years the little show had grossed something over a quarter of a million pounds I believe and Sir Oswald Stoll booked it for one week at the Alhambra Theatre, bang in the middle of London's West End.

We'd played Islington, but never the West End. It was our big chance.

We only had ten chorus girls. "They'll look lost on that big stage," I said. "We shall need another six at least."

"Are you crazy?" replied Archie. "This is only for one week. My company's been all right up to now. You can have two more, that's plenty."

"Then there's the dresses, Archie. They're too shabby for the Alhambra."

He stared. "For just one week I should hire a new company and get new dresses?"

"All right," I said with a shrug, "I'll make 'em all myself." I did, and I drilled the chorus. When it was fine I took them out in a charabanc to the country and drilled them in the fields.

Archie was busy preparing a set of "Rules of Behaviour" for when we reached the West End. He was convinced it was a den of vice. But all we girls were sure there would be crowds of millionaires and dukes waiting for us.

"Ladies of the company must beware of men at the stage door with flowers and invitations to dinner."

We were all thrilled when we read this one. Betty and the other girls were agog at the idea of gentlemen with expensive bouquets waiting to sweep us off to restaurants.

But all we saw were a bunch of cissy boys.

Don't think I'm sneering at Archie. I believed all these things just as much as he did. We all did. We must have been the simplest lot that ever wandered goggle-eyed into the dressing-rooms of a West End theatre.

We were all in the show, Betty, Edie, young Tommy and me. We begged Mum not to come up from Islington for the First Night. We had nerves enough as it was.

Just before the curtain went up a telegram came for me. That nearly finished me off. I'd never had a telegram before. I tore it open. It said: "Good luck and God bless you. Evelyn Laye."

Evelyn Laye! She was a tremendous star. Fancy her sending me a telegram! After that I was practically too nervous to go on at all.

When it was over we all went home to Islington on the top of a bus.

Next morning when the papers came, all I was concerned about was whether they'd liked the costumes I'd made for the chorus, and the dances I'd drilled into them.

"Brilliantly drilled . . . brilliantly dressed . . ." they said, and I'd never sewn a thing in my life before. I purred.

It wasn't until Archie, Bert, and Annie Lipman burst in waving handfuls of papers at me that I realised the show was a smash hit, and me too.

"But the dresses I made," I said delightedly to Archie. "Look what they said about my costumes!"

Archie gazed at me in horror. "You're the leading lady . . . the star," he said. "Don't you dare tell anyone you made those costumes."

I was the leading lady . . . the star.

Mum sat in her kitchen over the sweet-shop in Islington High Street and listened to us all. She was forty-six and I was twenty-seven. It had taken her twenty-seven years from that one room above Chip Sarah's fish shop in Rochdale. Twenty-seven years of "going 'oop." But today *all* her kids were actors, all on the stage, and in London.

"When d'you want to come and see us, Mum?" we asked. "We'll get you seats in the front row for tonight."

"Aye," said Jenny. "Well, I'll tell you when I'm ready."

We thought she was annoyed that we'd asked her not to come for the First Night.

The second night Archie splashed out in celebration. As there were six of us, Betty and her husband, Roy Parry, Edie, Tommy, Archie and me to go home to Islington he decided we could hire a car. It was a Daimler. We were thrilled.

I was the last to come out of the stage door. As I did two people approached me Shades of Archie's Rules flashed through my mind and I wondered for a moment what they were after.

"Miss Fields?" they asked.

"Aye," I said, warily.

They held out two books: "Would you sign these for us, please?"

"What for . . . *me* . . . oh . . ." I began.

AUTOBIOGRAPHY OF GRACIE FIELDS

Then it dawned on me, I was being asked for autographs! I was so nervous that I splashed ink everywhere as I shakily scrawled my name.

Through the windows of the Daimler I could see Betty, Edie and the lot of them falling about with laughter. I finished my signing, tripped over the step of the Daimler and fell in head first.

We couldn't wait to tell Jenny. *Autographs!*

When we got home she wasn't there. We were shocked. The pot was on the stove for supper. Dad, who had to go to work early, was sound asleep. There was no sign of Mum. We'd never known her to be out before when we got home. Just as we were getting panicky she walked in.

"Where've you been?" we clamoured.

"To see t'show."

"But you could have come home in the car with us, and we *told* you we'd get you the best seat."

"Ah came home on t'bus, and ah've had the best seat of the lot."

"Where?"

"In t'gallery," said Jenny, taking off her hat. "Where I could hear what folks said."

"What did they say?"

"Never mind," said Jenny, busying herself with the stew-pot.

"Our Grace was asked for her autograph!" said Betty, breaking the big news of the evening.

It was then that Jenny turned and smiled at all of us. "I know," she said simply. "I were there."

55

3

I HAD a twenty-five minutes' wait off-stage between two sketches in *Mr. Tower of London.* Sir Oswald Stoll, one of the biggest impresarios the theatre has known asked me if, in that wait, I could run across the street from the Alhambra Theatre to the Coliseum to do a ten-minute act there on my own.

I did it, and he paid me a cheque for one hundred pounds for the week.

Up to now I'd been earning at the most about twenty-eight pounds a week. In fact it wasn't all that long ago that I'd proudly told Jenny I'd got twenty pounds in the savings bank, and, for the first time in my life, I'd seen her eyes fill with tears. In all the struggle I don't think any of us had ever expected to be able to save the vast sum of twenty pounds. Now I had a piece of paper which said "Pay Gracie Fields one hundred pounds" signed "Oswald Stoll."

That cheque was the first hundred pounds I'd earned, by myself, in London's West End. I wanted to frame it.

"You can't do that," said Archie crossly. "If you don't put it in the bank, you won't get the money."

"And framing things like that is downright dangerous," said Jenny who still couldn't quite believe her eyes. "Having a hundred pounds stuck on t'wall! It'll encourage burglars!"

All of us were too ignorant to know that we could have asked Sir Oswald for another, stopped cheque, to frame. It was paid into the bank.

After that it all happened very quickly. We went 'oop! With a bang.

Within eighteen months Archie was a real impresario himself with five or six touring companies on the road, one starring Betty, one with Edie and Duggie Wakefield, another with Tommy, and me topping the variety bills in London on my own.

His brother, Bert Aza, was managing all of us, and Annie Lipman had become secretary and sort of Number One to Archie.

Yet for me life hadn't changed much. I still did all I was told to do and worked all the time. I still didn't know anyone outside the family. Archie and Bert met all the people. It suited me, I was too shy to know what to say to strangers.

Then one night an engraved calling card was sent to my dressing-room. "Sir Gerald du Maurier" it said, and scribbled under the name was the message: "I would like to see you."

I was twenty-nine and, in my mind, there were four beings of tremendous importance: God, the King and Queen, and the Mayor of Rochdale, in that order.

I read the name *Sir* Gerald du Maurier, and I reckoned that he must be even more important than the Mayor.

"Better tell 'em to coom in, luv," I said to Auntie Margaret, my mother's cousin, who was dressing me in the theatre.

Sir Gerald was the most important and most successful actor-manager in London then. His theatre, the St. James's, *the* most *élite* visited by Royalty and reserved for actors and actresses of great distinction and quite beautiful diction.

Now he stood in my dressing-room and told me he wanted *me* to be his leading lady in his next play.

"ME?" I gawped at him.

"Yes," said Sir Gerald, smiling the smile that had every actress in London in love with him. "I want you to play the part of Lady Weir in *S.O.S.*"

I thought he was barmy.

"Look," I said. "If it's a Lady Thingummy-bob you want me to play, ah'd have to talk posh, wouldn't I?"

"You'd have to talk in your normal voice," he agreed.

"But I've never used what you call a 'natural voice' on the stage in me life," I tried to explain. "I've always talked funny, exaggerated my accent, clowned it. I don't think I could talk all la-de-dah for very long. Still, how big is the part?"

"I'll send it to you tomorrow."

"Right," I said. "I'll measure it."

"*Measure* it?" said Sir Gerald.

"Yes, I'll measure the speeches; if they're not too long, I know I'll be able to keep up the right sort of voice without dropping back into Lancashire."

Two days later I got ready to see Sir Gerald again. Edie, the "proper" one of our family, did her best to dress me for this important appointment.

Just when she finally approved of me I tore upstairs and changed back into everything she had said I *shouldn't* wear. I put on my favourite scarlet and emerald tartan kilt, my purple Hungarian blouse, my fur coat and my Scots tammy.

"Why?" demanded my family.

"I didn't feel myself," I explained. "I couldn't stand it, all dressed up like that. I'd rather he saw me as I really am."

When he did see me Sir Gerald nearly dropped dead.

After a long silence he began to walk round and round me saying softly: "Good God! . . . Good God! . . . Good God! . . . Why a kilt?"

"I like 'em."

"And—the—er—blouse?"

"I like that too. I like anything with a bit of colour." I was beginning to feel uncomfortable. " 'Ere," I said, holding out the script to take his mind off my get-up, "ah've measured my part. I can do it."

Sir Gerald collapsed into a chair and let himself laugh. "All right," he said. "Come for your first rehearsal tomorrow."

When I got to the St. James's Theatre quite a lot of people whose faces I'd seen in the papers were there, among them Gladys Cooper, and Tallulah Bankhead sitting on a chair right in the middle of the stage. She said huskily, "Do you mind, dahling? I love to watch people closely at rehearsals."

No one had ever watched me rehearse before, but perhaps they did this in the West End. I didn't know, but I felt sick with nervousness.

The first thing Sir Gerald had to do in the play was to lead me to a chair and ask: "Are you all right, darling?" He did that, then he bent down and gave me a long sloppy kiss. The kiss wasn't in the script. I didn't know what to do. I fished for my hanky and blew my nose heartily to cover my embarrassment and to wipe my mouth. There was a rustle of amusement from the watching actresses, and I felt terrible.

Doggedly I la-de-dahed my way through Lady Weir's lines till the end. Then Sir Gerald bowed and the actresses clapped. I was going to play the part.

He introduced me to Viola Tree and asked her to take

59

me to see a genuine society Duchess who was running a dress shop in the West End.

"Half an hour of hearing *her* talk will do for Gracie," he said. "She'll have her off to a tee!"

The Duchess in question suffered from a weak heart, and so did the heroine in the play. I watched her very carefully in her shop, noticed her fluttering movements, the affected little mannerisms, listened to her mincing Mayfair drawl.

Then I went back to Sir Gerald and faithfully mimicked it all. He nearly had hysterics. "That's her, to the life!" he gasped between laughter. "But you're turning the play into a farce. Do it your own way." And I had to un-learn everything I'd copied so earnestly.

Next day Sir Gerald asked me to dine at his home with Lady du Maurier and their three daughters. They were charming to me but after the meal they left us alone to rehearse and, as soon as they'd gone, Sir Gerald put his arms round me and kissed me again.

I didn't like to push him away, but, when he'd done I said "Ee lad, don't be soft, you're older than me dad!" To my horror tears filled his eyes.

He was a highly emotional gifted actor, adored by women, and, as his daughter Daphne explains in her biography of him, he had a naïve charming vanity which made the loss of his youth unbearable to him. I didn't understand this at the time. When I heard smart actresses saying to him, "Gerald, darling, you don't look a day over thirty," I'd say innocently, "They're real daft, aren't they? You *do*, you know!" And he would laugh then because he liked my honesty.

He got used to my comments and when he gave me a picture of himself he signed it: "To Gracie, from Old du Maurier," and then took me out to lunch at the Green

Park Hotel where a posy of flowers and a little jade bauble were waiting for me beside my plate.

We had lunch together every Wednesday after that and always, beside my plate, was a little present, a bottle of perfume, a lace hanky, some flowers. Nothing so romantic had ever happened to me before and I began to wish he *was* thirty!

He taught me many things, and he paid me a very great compliment.

King George V had been to see us in S.O.S. Sir Gerald was invited to the Royal box afterwards and asked: "Now tell me, why did you choose Gracie Fields to be your leading lady? I've got some of her gramophone records and I like them, but I wouldn't have thought of her in a straight play."

Gerald told me he'd answered: "I think, Your Majesty, I chose her because there is something refreshing and sincere about her. This play's a tragedy, but it takes a great comédienne to play great tragedy."

The King stroked his beard for a moment. "Yes," he said, reflectively, "Yes, du Maurier, I think I know what you mean." A few weeks later I received a command—the first of many—to appear in the Variety Artistes' Royal Command Performance.

This was an honour to the work which Archie and Bert had said I should never leave—vaudeville. They had been against my acceptance of a part in a straight play and had kept arguing with me that my own work, in variety, where I belonged, would suffer.

Because they worried about this so much they arranged with Sir Gerald that, as Lady Weir "died" in the first hour of the play, I could leave S.O.S. each night in time to do the second house music hall at the Alhambra. From there I went on to the Café Royal and did a late night cabaret.

I was earning £100 at the St. James's, £200 at the Alhambra, and £300 at the Café Royal, and making gramophone records during the day.

Sir Gerald was amazed at all this work and couldn't understand it.

"I belong to music hall," I tried to explain. "I feel at home there. I know what I'm up to, giving folks a bit of a song and a laugh."

"Gracie," he asked me, "are you ever going to change your way of speaking . . . start to talk posh as you call it, all the time?"

I shook my head. "I think it's daft," I said, "and I'd only put my foot in it. I haven't had education like you, so I'll stay as I am. Why try to change?"

He looked at me seriously. "Grace, you're a lucky girl. I wonder if you know just how lucky? You have enough in you not to *have* to change, you *can* stay as you are."

"Aye," I thought, "we've all gone up in the world, just like me mumma said we were going to . . . but will it alter us?"

"You can stay just as you are," Sir Gerald had said—but could we? I hoped we could because I didn't know *how* to change, but with all that money I was earning, the fantastic sums I was going to earn, other people were changing.

When Archie started planning a fifteen thousand pound house in Hampstead with twenty-eight rooms in it; when Mum turned to Dad and said, "Oh, shut 'oop! You mak' us sound so common!"; and when my gay, lovely sister Betty stamped her feet despairingly and burst out with "Oh, Grace, you don't know, you don't *know* how *hard* I pray to God every night not to let me be jealous of my sister," I began to get lonely and frightened.

I had never been educated to meet the situation they call

fame, either at school, or by life, and it got me in a right proper muddle for a bit.

School had been something to be sandwiched between helping Jenny do the actors' washing, singing at smoking concerts, going off with Juvenile Troupes, or working in the mills, and I'd left at twelve anyway.

Life had been poverty and Jenny's consuming ambition that I should go on the stage, the stage meaning for me an unending succession of third-rate theatres and fifth-rate theatrical digs, for years, since I was seven, since I was fourteen, since I was twenty-one.

Now I was twenty-nine and suddenly, from never enough money, we had a ton of it, and everything I was doing brought in more.

Archie called this being famous. Perhaps because I was so shy and ill-at-ease with the posh people he, and Bert, and Annie Lipman all seemed to meet and know now, I never realised it as fame. But Archie did, and he was determined we should live up to it.

We had to stop living in homely comfortable places like Balham and Islington and move into this red-stoned mansion in Hampstead.

Fred, my dad, came to see it, pushed his hat to the back of his head and grunted: "What are you building, lass—a maternity home?" for it looked enormous. He didn't know what to think of it by the time the twenty-eight rooms were furnished and equipped, and neither did I.

The architect had devised a foundation stone inscribed: "Archie and Gracie." When he showed it to me I think he hoped I would burst into "God Bless Our Home." But the last thing "The Towers," as Archie called it, reminded me of was a home, it was more like a hotel.

It was furnished with a marble bathroom for every bedroom; an elevator with gold lacquered grilles; heavy crystal chandeliers in the mauve and gold reception rooms, and in the enormous mauve and gold ballroom, and leading to all this splendour was the real finale of the pantomime scene, a magnificent balustraded staircase.

In fact I felt a bit like Cinderella when I got home at nights and found a Russian princess poised at the foot of this staircase, smoking a cigarette in the longest holder I'd ever seen, and waiting to greet me. Archie had engaged her as a housekeeper to show us how to manage and how to live in style in our "palace." But to me the one thing you *couldn't* do in "The Towers" was to live in it.

Archie engaged a butler. I'd only seen butlers as pompous characters on the stage . . . the ones I always had to trip up, or pour the soup over. I'd never have dared pour the soup over the butler Archie got for us, he terrified me.

It was the same with the cooks. Archie hired two of them and you couldn't even go into your own kitchen to make a cup of tea.

Even the gardens, two acres of them, reminded you of a park. Archie bought squirrels to be released among the trees; we had five Airedales and two Kerry Blues in the kennels and indoors lived Annie Lipman's Pekinese and a parrot called Mac.

Archie strolled through all this magnificence in Sulka silk dressing gowns with his initials monogrammed on the pocket, enjoying every minute of it. I hated all of it and retreated to my own little sitting-room which I had insisted on furnishing myself. I'd made it as gay and cheerful as I could, it was homely and comfortable, and I spent nearly all my spare time there.

I suppose this was really the beginning of the break-up in my marriage to Archie.

It had been a partnership of convenience and long association. We had come a long way together and, with

Archie's help and constant dominance over me, we had reached fame. But our ways of accepting it were different. Archie could, and did live up to it; in one year he changed his car eight times. I couldn't, and even trying to made me miserable.

I looked at the other stars and regarded them as beings from another world, a world in which I could never take a place. *imposter syndrome*

This was no mock modesty. I hadn't the faintest idea of how to behave or look like Gertrude Lawrence, Tallulah Bankhead, Gladys Cooper or any of the other great names, and their sophisticated lives terrified me.

When I had a chauffeur-driven car for the theatre I felt uncomfortable at the thought of keeping the driver waiting all that time for me till the show ended. I used to send him off and go home by bus. This sort of thing made Archie mad.

Perhaps the best example of the differences which grew between us was the little ramshackle cottage he bought for me. It was on the borders of the Devonshire and Cornish coasts, at Cawsand Bay, just outside Plymouth. I'd seen and fallen in love with it when we were there on tour.

Archie's gift had touched me. The cottage was the first property I'd ever owned in my life, and I was so proud of it that I carried its key in my bag everywhere I went. I made plans for furnishing it with cottagey things, and spending holidays there.

Some time later I was appearing again at Plymouth. I'd told everybody in the company about my cottage and arranged a picnic for them all to come and see it.

When we got there there was no cottage—only a bare patch of ground.

From Plymouth I phoned Archie in London: "Archie, somebody's pulled my cottage down!"

"Yes," he said, surprised at my distress, "I did. You can't have an old dilapidated place like that. I'm going to build a modern house there with a fine garden and . . ."

"No," I said miserably, "no, Archie, you don't understand. Do what you like with it. I don't want it now."

"Oh, really, Grace!" he said impatiently, and hung up.

His brother Bert Aza was a more gentle person, and with much more understanding. As my manager he too had his problems with me, but he always seemed to know how to handle them.

At this time my fan mail, which came in sack loads, began to worry me. Begging letters were a nightmare.

Once I was in Bert's office reading some. I told his secretary: "Send a cheque to this one." Bert pricked up his ears. "Give it to me," he said.

"No, Bert, this one's genuine. I'd like to send her some money."

"Not one in a thousand is genuine," said Bert. "If you sent only half the money they ask for it would cost you ten thousand pounds a week."

"But surely it wouldn't hurt to send this one three pounds." It was from a poor old woman who told me she would be sent to prison if she didn't pay her milk bill.

Bert sighed. "I'll tell you what, I'll get a detective to investigate. If it's genuine I shall give her a tenner myself. There, now will that do you?"

The detective's report came in two days later. The poor old woman was a healthy young man who drove a sports car!

In the end Archie and Bert insisted that they deal with most of the letters, and after that they gave me only those they thought would interest me.

I couldn't see why folks should write so much to somebody they had only seen on the stage, or heard on the wire-

random dynamic

less. I didn't know them as people, but I began to know them as audiences, and their generous letters made me aware of a wonderful human warmth surging out to me whenever I sang.

Amid all the new impersonal richness of the mansion I had to call home, the work, the success, those letters were comforting. My new loneliness would have been deeper without them. That fan mail and those audiences were like something warm and good—it was like being loved. The only place then that seemed like home was the middle of the stage; *that* didn't change.

I suppose, in a funny way, I was homesick. All my life my family have mattered more than anything in the world to me, and all my life till now I had lived close to them. Home was with Dad and Mum round the kitchen fire in Rochdale and Islington; work was with Betty, Edith, Tommy, Archie and Bert, always together.

Now Betty was married and had a flat of her own. Edith had married comedian Duggie Wakefield and had eventually given up the stage, which she had always hated for herself. Tommy was in the theatre on his own And I had persuaded Dad to give up working, and bought a house for him and Mumma in Peacehaven, just outside Brighton.

We'd all been for a charabanc ride round Brighton one day and someone had said: "Reckon this'd be a nice place for you to keep a few chickens, Fred." Dad reckoned it would, and Mum thought somewhere near Brighton would be a good place for all of us to come at week-ends.

They settled in there for only a few weeks before Mum announced that she felt banished, and Dad said it was too far from a pub. So we got another house nearer the main road, the buses, Brighton, *and* a pub. Then the picnic began.

Before Mum had finished with that house it had grown

67

a couple of wings. Betty and Roy Parry had a son, so Mum added a room for him. Edith and Duggie had a son, then a daughter, so Mum added a room for them. Then she got a couple of maids, and built a room for each of *them*.

We all went home to Peacehaven most week-ends, and every time we found that Mum had been visiting the neighbours during the week. "Ee, they've got a lovely garden path, Grace, you must come and see it."

"Yes, Mumma, it is lovely, but we've *got* a lovely garden path. New. Hardly walked on."

"Aye; but it's not as nice as theirs."

Next time I'd go down there'd be a new path, just like the neighbours'.

"We ought to have a tennis court, Grace," said Jenny, firmly.

"No, Mumma, none of us play tennis."

We got the tennis court. Dad kept his chickens on it.

She saw someone's goldfish pond. "Ah'll make one like that meself," said Dad.

Next time I arrived he led me to the top of the garden. "Ah got carried away," he explained, peering down the gaping great cavern in front of us. "It went proper deep."

"Deep enough for a swimming pool," said Jenny.

We made it into a swimming pool. Then we got terrified that the babies would fall in so we filled it up with muck. It stayed that way till one hot summer's day when someone said they must have a swim, so we heaved all the muck out again, and put a boat on the water.

I was sitting by the pool, all fancy on a chaise-longue with my feet up, when Dad arrived home from the pub full of beer and benevolence and beamed at me: "This is the life, Grace! Ooo-HO! a life on the ocean wave!" He put one foot in the boat and sank base over apex to the bottom. I had to jump in with all my clothes on to rescue him.

After that we had rails and a couple of lifebelts put round our private ocean, and it was never warm enough to go swimming in it again!

Workmen never seemed to leave Peacehaven, and I'm not surprised. Mum was in her glory, she played them concerts of all my records, gave them full course regular meals, and always found something new for them to do as soon as they'd finished the last thing.

My manager, Bert Aza, who had been a bit stunned by some of the construction bills that came in, went down to have a look to see if we were re-building the whole town!

He came back with his eyes popping out of his head. "What's she doing with that army of workmen?" he demanded. "Their foreman came in to inquire if the men had finished their fruit and cream yet!"

I put my foot in it finally when I went to a famous London furnishing store to ask them to send some things down for one of the reception rooms. "I want them for the Fatty-Do room," I explained, using my dad's name for the room you always kept right to ask people in.

When the elegant young man from the store arrived on Mum's doorstep she received him with her best lady-of-the-manor air only to be told with great solemnity: "I've come about the Fatty-Do room, Mrs. Stansfield."

"That's our Grace," said Mum, with exasperation, "she never will stop making us all sound real daft!"

I lived for the week-ends that I could get down to Peacehaven. This was the fun of "going 'oop."

I didn't care, and I didn't have to care how many rooms and paths and pools and tennis courts Mum built. The place was home, filled with people, noise, laughter and kids! Dozens of kids for, in addition to my own small nephews and niece, I'd now got an orphanage.

I'd had the first house that I'd bought for Mum and Dad

on my hands at a time when Lottie Albert, the secretary of
the Theatrical Ladies' Guild, was at her wits' end to find
room for the children of actors who had either died, or were
having hard times.

"Why not use our old house?" I'd asked her, and she had
jumped at it. So the house was called "The Gracie Fields
Home and Orphanage" and it was run by Lottie and the
Guild.

It was so near our new home at Peacehaven that I could
pop over to it whenever I wanted, and I wanted to do that
a lot. *can she have kids?*

Neither Mum nor I could ever resist kids, so we took to
inviting them up to our place. There were only eight of
them to begin with, but gradually we made the orphanage
big enough to take twenty-five, and I reckon I must have
hundreds of adopted nieces and nephews calling me
"Auntie Grace" since then. My own little niece once asked
me wonderingly: "Do you know all the children in the
world, Auntie Grace?"

Though I've made a fortune in my time I don't know
much about stocks and shares and such like to this day. But
if you ask me about good investments I can tell you that
the few thousands that house cost me, and the bits and
pieces that have gone into it since, have been the best investment I ever made.

I haven't been able to have children of my own but the
orphanage has given me a never-ending family, and in Canada, America, all over, all through my life, boys and·girls
have turned up beaming at me: "Hallo, Auntie Grace, remember me? I was one of your children."

And they say that money doesn't buy happiness. That's
rubbish; it can, if you know the right way to go about it.
But it took me rather a long time to find that out.

This was the difficult time for me, and I was all muddled

70

up. It seemed to me real daft to have to live my own life in a mauve and gold chocolate box of a house, bossed around by servants, and always frightened of saying the wrong thing.

Archie said I should have a mink coat, and I was so nervous when I wrote out such a big cheque for a coat that I made a real mess of it, and had to write it out three times before it could be understood. *anti-glamour* *

Then Archie said I should have a Rolls Royce. I felt as though I was going to work in a hearse.

I loved pottering around in Woolworths, but I got stopped from doing that because so many people gathered around me they had to call the police.

All the big-wigs asked me to join their charity do's. I liked the things they were working for, but I'd rather have sung a song than have to go through the ordeal of having dinners with them. I dreaded the events for days.

I went to one big dinner one night, and saw the host, a Lord somebody, breaking up his bread and putting it in his soup. I was so astonished that I blurted out: "They told me never to do that, but *you're* doing it!"

He was sensible that chap. "Good Lord, don't mind what 'they' say," he told me. "If you like bread in your soup, and I do, put the blasted bread in."

I put the blasted bread in. It seemed easy after that. I've done it ever since.

That small incident meant a lot to me. I began to realise dimly that perhaps I didn't have to endure all this Rolls Royce and mink nonsense and live in a "gilded cage."

Then my sister Betty introduced me to two men who completed my education, gave me the courage of my own common sense, and altered the whole of my life. One was a writer called Henry Savage, and the other an artist, John Flanagan.

71

It was while I was doing my three hundred pounds a week cabaret turn at the Café Royal. I sang upstairs in the ritzy part, but downstairs was the café where all the artistic crowd gathered; people like Epstein and Augustus John were regular patrons.

Betty and her artist husband, Roy Parry, often used to go there, and one night Betty swept me down to meet some people.

"This is Henry and this is John," she announced, "and John wants to paint you."

Henry, the writer, a small clever man with a big nose and very kind eyes murmured a greeting, John, the painter, just stared. He was an Irishman with curly black hair and the saddest face I'd ever seen. Now he gazed at me with all the combined pensiveness of good whisky and his Irish nature, and then confirmed in melancholy tones: "I see much in your face that I would like to paint."

I blushed, Betty giggled, and Henry Savage who was stroking a tiny tea-coloured kitten blinked up at me humourously.

"Well don't blush, Grace," said Betty, "sit down and let him have a good look at you in comfort."

Normally I would have felt too stupid, but these people didn't make me feel self-conscious. They didn't seem to be waiting for me to say something funny as most people did, they just went on talking. They talked about books I'd never heard of, places I'd never seen. By the time we went home I'd agreed to go to John Flanagan's studio to sit for him.

He lived and worked in a studio up a quiet back lane in St. John's Wood; it was full of the usual untidy bric-à-brac of an artist, happy-go-lucky and friendly. It was the homeliest place I'd come across in London.

Auntie Margaret, my cousin and dresser, usually came

where is the painting now?

along with me, and John always had Henry Savage there. Auntie Margaret is real Lancashire, and homely, too. We made a good foursome.

John and Henry talked endlessly at the sittings. They had no condescension for my ignorance, rather, it seemed to me, a real pleasure in being able to introduce me to the surprise and delight of books, poetry and painting. They lent me books. Often they gave me small presents, curios, pottery, paintings they had picked up for a few shillings in the Caledonian market. They showed me how these things were beautiful, how to look for the craftsman's work and skill hidden in them.

I began to see what I had missed by leaving school at twelve, and, best of all, that I could still catch up. Before, when I was alone, I had just sat and played endless gramophone records. Now I read and read, greedy for all the things I'd missed. But I felt more of a prisoner than ever in my marble hall of a home. And Archie and I began having quarrels. I'd been so used to doing everything he told me that I felt guilty and even disloyal every time I "disobeyed." I even got into trouble because I would walk up the stairs instead of using the fancy gold lift—I just couldn't use that lift somehow. *rebels against celeb perks*

One day I went for a sitting to John's studio and he said excitedly: "Henry and I are going to the South of France."

"When?" I asked.

His face fell. "That's the trouble, it's your damned portrait. I can't finish it, and I can't leave it alone. Something about your face baffles me. On the stage you're all alive, you're bubbling, everyone wants to feel the way you're obviously feeling. Yet when you come here . . ." he shrugged helplessly, "You smile, but your eyes always look miserable, half dead."

I was embarrassed. We never discussed feelings in our

family; I didn't know what to say, but I knew what he meant.

"You've got a rich home, you make piles of money, you're on top of the world, you can't do anything wrong, yet when I try to catch some of those sparks you give off when you're working I can't, they're not there. What the hell's the matter with you?" he ended angrily. And I burst out crying.

All the things which had been stored up for so long came out . . . how I couldn't live up to it all, how everything had changed, the bewilderment, the shyness, the awful feeling of not belonging anywhere any more. "Sometimes I'm even frightened that my family will change. . . ." It all came out, more than I'd thought was in me to tell.

John heard me out. "What am I going to do?" I said, desperately ashamed of my outburst, but glad I'd got it off my chest.

"Easy!" said John. "Pack! Leave 'The Towers' and all its trimmings, leave everything for a bit, pack a bag and come to France with Henry and me. I'll chaperone Henry, and he'll chaperone me. Not that we need it. Come away with you, girl, fold up your tent!"

But I didn't, and neither did they, for a bit. It was just about this time that I realised I really *was* famous, and John became ill.

He worried me. His studio was very cold, and he wasn't much of a one for taking care of himself, and Henry wasn't much of a nurse.

This pair had become my friends. I treated them as I would have treated anyone in our street in Rochdale, and they treated me the same way. Auntie Margaret and I took to going over on the bus after the show to see that they had got in enough milk and things in the place, and that there was a good fire banked-up for the night.

John was still very ill when I was asked to do a terrifying

74

thing. A show heralded to open at the Gaiety Theatre with all the boost and publicity of a *My Fair Lady* was called *Topsy and Eva*. It was to star the very famous American Duncan sisters.

A week after a fantastic opening the sister playing Topsy was rushed to hospital. They asked me to take her part.

While the newspaper headlines screamed out the news I sat up all night with a vinegar bandage round my head trying to learn the complicated lines, dances and songs. I nearly went crazy, and was so nervous that I got a stiff neck, so stiff that I couldn't turn my head at all.

I rehearsed all that night, and all the next day, while the publicity went on and on.

As I stood in the wings, my neck still rigid with pain, waiting to give the saucy laugh which had to ring out before I appeared, I wondered if I'd even get a croak out. Then bingo! the laugh came, the stiff neck vanished, and I bounced on to the stage.

At the end there was such an ovation I thought the roof would fall in.

When I finally got out of the stage door, dressed in my inevitable kilt and raincoat, I thought there was a fire or something. The street was jammed solid with people—and then they began to cheer.

I didn't grasp that they were cheering me until I found myself on their shoulders, and had to stay there, jostled and patted, cheered and chaired down the whole length of the Strand.

Even as I remember it now I can still scarcely believe it, but I can remember how I felt sitting on the shoulders of that great crowd, bobbing down the brightly-lit street with the traffic stopped and people yelling "Our Gracie! Our Gracie!" I was all mixed up with pride, tears, bewilderment, happiness and just not knowing how to begin to say thank you, or to tell folks that it was all too much.

But when they put me down, and Betty and everyone rushed up with hugs and congratulations and a dozen invitations to important parties, I managed to get Betty on one side.

"Betty," I said, "I can't go to any of the parties. I've promised to go to the Studio to bank-up the fire for John. If I don't he'll let it go out, and then he'll get worse."

I wasn't in love with John Flanagan, nor he with me, and my sister knew it, but he was my friend, and he was ill. Betty stood there, breathless, excited, her red curls tumbled about her face, her eyes shining. Then she drew a deep breath. I thought she was going to go for me for being so stupid.

Instead, in a rush of words, just like when she was a little girl, she said, "Oh! God really *did* choose to give the success to the right sister. Grace, I'd have just *had* to go, to *all* the parties, there couldn't have been enough for me."

"You go, Betty," I said. "You go."

But Betty shook her head. "No, luv," she said quickly. "No, I'm coming with you."

I couldn't say more. We'd all been brought up not to be demonstrative. "Don't be sloppy," Mum had always said.

But for that childish habit of not "being sloppy" I would have hugged my sister, and cried then. I love her very much, but I don't think I have ever loved her more than in that moment when, with all the tremendous generosity of her honesty, she gave me the two things I'd been looking for . . . the knowledge that I didn't have to change because I was famous, and that I didn't have to change for my own family either. They'd get used to this "fame" business, just as I should, but they'd go on loving me just the way I was.

When Betty and I left the crowds and got to John's

studio to bank-up the fire, he grumbled at me: "Of course, you would have to come here looking like that just when I can't get up to work."

"Looking like what?" I said. "You know damned well," said John in a surly voice, "you're alive again."

"Yes," I said to him. "In fact I might even pack up my bags and come to the South of France with you and Henry!"

As soon as he was better they went off to Cannes, and London became empty again for me. It was just work, songs, rehearsals and bed. Then, two days before the opening of our new revue *The Show's The Thing* I had a blazing quarrel with Archie.

That very morning John and Henry had sent me a picture postcard from Cannes and on it they'd written: "Don't stay there and have a nervous breakdown. Come here and have a holiday, your understudy will be delighted."

Despite all my unhappiness I had never once thought of rebelling against Archie's rule. Since I had been fifteen it had been my habit to obey him. I did what he told me in the theatre, I did what he told me in the gaudy palace of a place he'd chosen as our home.

grooming

That morning I felt I could stand it no longer. I went to find Betty. "I know I shouldn't leave the show," I said. "I know he'll be furious, but I'm so unhappy, Betty, I don't think I can stand it another minute."

As none of us was much given to showing our feelings, this was a big confession for me to make to my sister. But she must have seen that I was nearly at breaking point. She backed me up. "Go on, luv," she said, "please yourself for once. You go."

I packed a small case quickly, and feeling like a criminal, I got a taxi to Victoria station and caught the boat-train for France.

But I didn't know any sense of freedom or release as I sat in the train. On the cross-channel boat I felt even worse. What had I done? I'd let them all down, I'd run away, been cowardly. I should have stayed behind and had things out with Archie, once and for all.

As soon as I got to Paris I telephoned London to ask Betty if Archie had called the show off, or found another leading lady to replace me.

Her husband, Roy, answered the phone and he sounded miserable. "Betty's gone down to Peacehaven," he said, "but your brother Tommy's here."

They were both heartbroken because I'd gone. It was to have been Tommy's first big chance in the West End as one of the principal comedians. Roy had designed the scenery. They sounded all at sixes and sevens on the phone. No, they didn't know what was going to happen. No, no one had plucked up courage to talk to Archie yet. I found myself crying into the telephone. I knew there could be no good in running away, that wouldn't solve anything.

"Look, luv," I said to Tommy, "don't worry. I'm coming back, right away." Then I made myself phone Archie. "Please, Archie," I said. "I'm sorry—can I come back?"

"I never asked you to leave," he answered calmly. "You can come back if you wish."

When I got home, bedraggled and red-eyed off the midnight steamer, it was Annie Lipman who greeted me at the door of "The Towers."

Annie had started calling Archie "The Guv'nor" and now she said: "I knew you'd come back. I told the Guv'nor, 'she'll be back, don't worry'." And apparently he'd believed her. He had not made a single move to cover himself against my absence from the show. I'd never defied him, and he never really expected that I would.

I felt as though all the life had gone out of me as I went

back into the final rehearsals and I worked in a daze, but when we opened we had another big hit. *The Show's The Thing* ran for over a year in various West End theatres.

While we were at the Lyceum the great operatic diva, Madame Tetrazzini, came to see us. She sat in the first box and eyed me through pearl-handled lorgnettes.

I was on-stage playing my comedy role of maid to a newly-rich family, dressed in skivvy's cap and apron, all awry, with twisted black stockings full of holes.

"Did I ever tell you," one of the family dinner guests boomed pompously, "that my uncle was Lord Trum-trum and my father—ah—was Baron——."

"Pity yer mother wasn't——!" I interrupted.

The audience roared, and not only at the crack. They guessed what was likely to happen to those plates of soup I was juggling.

In the next scene I was a scrub-woman in greasy cap and apron, down on my knees swilling soapsuds and earthy jokes and getting shrieks of laughter.

Through all this Madame Tetrazzini sat straight and proud, a regal dark-haired little figure. She had one of the most beautiful and skilled singing voices in the world. Why did she come to a show like ours?

"What's she doing here?" I panted as I came off, but the answer was waiting for me. Apparently she had heard that although I came on-stage as a scrub-woman and clowned my way through half a dozen operatic arias in a mixture of Lancashire, Italian and French, I was getting all the top notes. Now she had sent a note round asking if I would sing the aria from *La Traviata* for her.

I was in a panic. I had never had a real singing lesson in my life and I had learnt all the arias from listening to the great Galli-Curci's records. Since I couldn't understand any of the Italian or French I'd freely mixed the phrases up

79

with comical gibberish, and then deliberately murdered them when I did them on-stage. It always brought the house down.

But I loved Grand Opera, and I loved Tetrazzini's voice too much to want to ridicule great music in front of her. Yet how could I sing it otherwise? To me opera was only for singers who were properly trained. I should have loved to have learnt, but when I had been young there had been no money for singing lessons, and now I understood too much about operatic music to dream of attempting to sing it unless I could do it perfectly.

There was only one thing to do, go on-stage and guy the aria she had requested, as I usually did. I went, but I was quaking.

I was so nervous that I started two tones too high, but the Lord was with me, and I hit every note truly. At the end of the song I was supposed to throw my charlady's wet cloth at the audience. As I came off Archie, who had been standing in the wings said, "You were singing straight at Tetrazzini, and my God! for a moment I thought you were going to throw the cloth at her too!"

"I was that nervous I didn't know where I was chucking it," I said. But when I got to my dressing-room the great singer was there waiting for me, and I saw there was no need to be nervous. Her big dark eyes were filled with tears. She was a little woman, and she stood on tip-toe and put up both her arms to embrace me. I wanted to cry too. I hugged her back, clumsily.

"My dear," she said, "oh, my dear, you *must* sing in opera, in good, great opera, not, not *this* . . ." and with a wave of her hand she dismissed the whole Lyceum theatre.

We had our photographs taken together, because she wanted it. And she autographed the gramophone disc of her own recording of Verdi's wonderful music for me, but she couldn't persuade me to leave the music hall for the opera house. I stayed where I knew I belonged, but I have always cherished the memory that a great artiste like Tetrazzini thought I had enough talent to train in her footsteps.

Eighteen months later, when *The Show's The Thing* ended, I told Archie that I must have a rest, and this time he didn't demur.

John and Henry were still urging me to go on that holiday to France with them, but I had a better idea. Edward Chapman who worked in revue with me had lent me a book called "South Wind" by Norman Douglas, all about a wonderful Mediterranean island. Although in the book the island is called "Nepenthe" it is, in fact, Capri, and it sounded like the place I'd been searching for.

Once I'd started to read books seriously my imagination had run riot. All the things I should have done in childhood, "living" every book I read, pretending to be the characters, pretending to go to all the places in my mind, were, instead, happening to me now. But with one big difference, I was no longer a child, and I was no longer poor. I *could* go to the places I read about, if I wanted to.

I read about far-away islands, and dreamed of them as golden places set under blue skies where sunshine spilled over flowers and woods, and I would be utterly happy—though how, or why, I didn't know.

Books on the South Sea Islands had fascinated me and for quite a while, after reading Somerset Maugham, I thought I'd like to live in Tahiti, though I decided that was a bit far. And then, in "South Wind" I read about Capri, and that gave me the idea that my dream island really existed.

I was a bit in need of a few dreams coming true.

It would be hypocritical to say that I was ever deeply in

love with Archie Pitt. I wasn't, nor he with me. But our marriage had been based on a professional partnership which, of itself, had given me a sense of closeness to him, and, like any young woman, I should have liked to have been in love.

I'd always had a dream of belonging to someone, not as the person I was on the stage, but as the person I was when I took the make-up off. The "someone" would understand exactly when I felt shy, or scared, when I felt I was plain and inadequate, and I knew, that just because he *would* understand, none of those things would ever bother me much again.

Well, that was the dream. The reality, with Archie, was just the opposite; and, as we became more successful, even the understanding that existed between us when the make-up was *on* disappeared. When our marriage disintegrated I felt as though I was a personal failure. It didn't seem right to go round being miserable when I had so much to be happy about; it seemed wicked, and ungrateful.

So I pushed the dream of a "someone" to the back of my mind and my heart for a long, long time, and I went to fall in love with an island instead, an island called Capri.

4

MY DECISION to please myself and go to find my Mediterranean dream island with my friends John Flanagan and Henry Savage was really the day that Grace Stansfield and Gracie Fields became one and the same person.

I had learned, at last, that Grace Stansfield, the Rochdale mill kid who liked fish and chips, and cups of cocoa, and people who weren't stuck-up, could go on liking them and enjoying them wherever she went as Gracie Fields.

You can get good fish and chips at the Savoy; and you can put up with the fancy people once you understand that you don't have to be like them.

If I wanted luxury I supposed I could buy it, but I could also enjoy it in my own way. I didn't *have* to conform to Archie's wishes all the time. I was old enough to be free to think, and do, as I wanted, and it was with that new-found realisation that I went off entirely on my own, for the first time in my life, to join John and Henry.

They were staying in a French village, the one painting, the other writing, till I arrived, full of my plans and eager to get on with them. "Come on," I said, "we don't want to hang about here, let's go and see Capri."

They were astonished enough that I'd plucked up courage to leave my work, and my "gilded cage" and join them, let alone that I now wanted to go to a remote Italian island.

"My passport is out of date," said John nervously—any kind of official document always paralysed John. "What will happen if the Italian authorities notice it?"

"I don't know," I said. "Let's go and find out." So we went, and a pretty odd trio we must have looked.

John and Henry always dressed how they liked, and that was very casually. I was wearing a skirt and blouse under an old mackintosh, but I carried a new week-end dressing case which was the last word in elegance. It didn't fit our style at all. Every policeman we met looked first at us, and then at the case, very thoughtfully.

Sure enough, when we reached the Italian border the Customs man glared at us, our odd outfits, my brand new suitcase and curtly demanded: "Passports!"

John went pale. Something had to be done. I *did* want to see Capri. I began to sing "Santa Lucia," one of the Italian songs I knew, and that did it. The Customs officer beamed: "Aaaaah! Artista!" To him that explained everything; he took the passports and stamped them without even looking at the dates. Artists were obviously crazy in anybody's language. In a few moments we were in our first Italian train.

None of us spoke a word of the language except Henry who had asked the train waiter how to say "Thank you," which is "Grazie."

The first town we stopped at seemed to be "Uscita." We all fussed over the map looking for it till a weary Roman gentleman sitting opposite said with heavy politeness: "Uscita iss Way Out!"

"Oh, grazie!" said Henry hastily.

He had an old overcoat far too warm for summer on the

Mediterranean, but it had a bit of moth-eaten fur lining of which Henry was very proud. We soon learned that when he carried the coat over his arm with the fur showing we were treated like eccentric millionaires, and sent to the best hotels. When he carried it with the threadbare tweed showing we were directed to the cheapest places. In this fashion we finally reached Naples and found the boat to Capri.

Now sometimes it can be a very dangerous thing to go in search of a dream for the reality does not always match it, and I think I was half afraid to see Capri.

We stayed at a small hotel near the harbour and hired a horse carriage to drive up and down the winding rocky roads.

Little white and pink villas clung to the grey mountainsides, and from the top of each hill you looked down on the sapphire blue sea. Lizards darted on the sunbaked walls, and every tree and bush showered their coloured scented petals over the island till the whole place seemed to be carpeted in flowers.

We went up to Anacapri, the higher part of the island made famous by Axel Munthe's "Story of San Michele"; we went down to the little town square or piazza and drank coffee and listened to the Italians chattering.

It was picturesque and lovely, but I had been sure that I would feel something special about this island, and as yet, I didn't. I was ready to leave and just to remember it as a beautiful place I had once seen.

John and Henry felt the same way, they were ready to go too, but our carriage driver wanted to take us down to the far side, to a place called "the little sea shore," the Marina Piccola.

"Oh, we don't want to see any more," grumbled John, but I insisted. "Might as well, while we're here," I said. "We may never come back again."

The horse clopped down a long, ever winding hill. There were few houses. For a while all you could see were the green pine trees, the sprawling flowers and small vineyards. And then we rounded the final curve in the steep hillside and saw a blue bay with cloud-capped mountains towering above it, and, it seemed to me, all the beauty of the island crowding to shelter and frame this one small cove in loveliness. *sense of coming home*

Then I knew that if only one blade of grass of this gentle, wonderful place could belong to me, I would be happy. This *was* the dream come true.

I couldn't explain it all to John and Henry, but I knew that I must stay longer in Capri. We clambered out of the carriage and I noticed a small sign on a low, rough, grey wall that bounded some sort of a house. In four languages it said: "Rooms to let."

We walked along a rough path towards a broken-down yard where a donkey brayed, two crazy-looking Alsatian dogs began barking their heads off, and a brood of chickens scattered, clucking wildly.

A woman came out from a long, low shanty-like shack that looked like a disused tramcar and gestured to us to wait. Then a middle-aged man appeared, followed by a youth of about sixteen who spoke some English. In a few minutes we had agreed to stay in the odd-looking place for a few days.

We discovered that the man was an Italian nobleman called the Marchese Patrizi, the woman was his wife, and the youth, Ettore, their son.

Though the lodgings we had with them were very comfortable we still got badly bitten by mosquitoes. I was not used to the foreign food constantly fried in oil and got violent indigestion, and, of course, I couldn't understand a word anyone said.

I'd never lived in a foreign country and I'd often felt homesick for Rochdale even when I was in London. Yet here, in this island, miles away from England, I felt at home and at peace. No one knew who I was, and no one cared just so long as you smiled at them and they could smile back.

We stayed with the Patrizis for ten days, then it began to rain, John and Henry got restless, and I had to go back to work anyway. They went back to their French village and I went back to London. But, before I left, I told young Ettore Patrizi "If ever there's a little house or a bit of land for sale round here, mind you let me know." And I left him my address. I couldn't quite believe that he ever would write to me, but I felt happier at leaving by having made some attempt to return.

Back in London the dream of living in a place like Capri seemed more impossible than ever, for Archie and Bert had started to put me into films, and *Sally in Our Alley* was the first one.

None of us knew anything about film making and the chaos of those first few weeks is something I shall never forget.

For a start I had to get up at six A.M. and I'd thought those sort of days, which began before dawn, had finished when I'd left the mill.

Then, after a tense and difficult drive with Archie who must have been pretty nervous himself, we got to the studios and the make-up man started on me. "I shall have to shave your upper lip." I asked why and he said, "You have some hair on it." "Have I?" I said, "I've never noticed it." "No," he replied, "but the camera will." I protested, he won, and then Maurice Elvey, who was directing, came to look at me and said I needn't have been shaved at all. That was a typical start to a day.

87

Basil Dean was producing and Archie was taking a hand in everything. We started with one small scene in which I had to greet a cab-driver with three words: "Good morning, George."

I said "Good morning, George" all that day, and all the next day. At the end of forty-eight hours we hadn't got beyond that one scene. In the end I was slyly directed by the camera man.

It was in this film that my signature tune, "Sally" was born, and Bill Haines, who helped to write it said that selling "Sally" to us was the luckiest break in his life.

Apparently very late one evening two writers, Harry Leon and Leo Towers, came to his office with a song called "Gypsy Sweetheart" which they wanted him to hear, and to buy, because they were both hard-up. Bill Haines wanted to sell a song too as he was having a bit of a struggle getting himself established.

He let them play it over and though he didn't like the title, he *did* like the first eight bars of the chorus. He kept them playing those first eight bars while he tried to think of a lyric. He started out with "Mary, Ma-ry" and finally ended up with "Sally, Sa-lly," got through as far as a line "when skies are blue you are smiling," and then got stuck for something to rhyme with "smiling."

Just then an old pal, half tight as usual, put his nose round the office door. Bill said, "Here, chum, quick, think of a good rhyme for 'smiling'," and the pal said simply: "Beguiling," whereupon Bill slipped him a dollar, told him to go straight home, and wrote the two lines: "When skies are blue you're beguiling. When they are grey you're still smiling, smiling."

The three boys then rang up music publisher Bert Feldman and asked him to listen to their new number "Sally." When they got to the Feldman office Bert said there were too many songs called "Sally" already, and anyway it was too late, and they'd have to bring it round to him again in the morning.

Leo Towers went home, and Bill Haines asked Harry Leon to go with him to the Metropolitan Theatre in Edgware Road to see the second house music hall. When they got there I was topping the bill.

I'd already recorded one song of Bill's, called "'Fonso," and he thought he might as well try "Sally" on me to see if I would do anything with it. As it happened I was taking requests from the audience that night and they'd just asked for "'Fonso" so when I knew Bill and Harry were there I asked them to come and see me.

"Let's hear the new one up in my dressing-room," I suggested, but when they sang it to me I didn't care for it much on first hearing. "I want another good comic song from you," I told Bill Haines. "I think 'Sally' is a number for a man to sing, I don't think it'd be much good for me. Now go on, buzz off. I've got to change me skirt for the next scene."

I'd no idea till long afterwards, when Bill had helped to write "Walter" and "The Biggest Aspidistra in the World" for me too, just how disconsolate they felt as I cheerfully sent them away. But, as soon as they'd gone, I remembered that the title of my first film was going to be *Sally in Our Alley*, and I yelled after them to come back.

"I'll tell Archie about it," I said, "and you get in touch with him, so don't show it to anyone else till you've spoken to him."

Archie asked Bill out to our house in Hampstead to play the number, and then didn't like the last line, so he told him to have a cup of tea and try to think of a better ending. Annie Lipman was there and it was she who produced the last words: "You're more than the whole world to me."

Finally, when Archie had an audition of several songs for the film, I sang "Sally" and Archie settled on it. None of us had any idea that it would become the song which has been linked with my name ever since, and least of all when we were doing it in the film.

I have sung "Sally" all over the world since, in peace and war, in triumph and disaster, but never in such nightmare conditions as that first time, in the film studio.

I was supposed to be in a coffee-house when I was singing, and to get what they called "the right smokey atmosphere" they decided to burn brown paper. The fumes made the technicians sneeze, and each time one of their muffled sneezes was picked up on the sound track we had to scrap that recording and start all over again.

I can't remember how many times we had to do it before it was recorded properly, but I can remember standing there, my eyes streaming with the smoke from the burning paper and the glare from the baking kleig lights, and all the camera, sound and lighting crews going red in the face and working like mad to get it all in the can before they either coughed or choked.

Somehow we finished that film and somehow, to my huge astonishment, it was a big success. I viewed this with very mixed feelings for it meant they wanted me to make more, and I had never disliked any work so much. The same chaotic conditions prevailed for the next one, *Looking on the Bright Side*. I'd get up at six, be made-up by nine, no one would get organised properly till eleven A.M. yet each night we would grind on, arguing and blundering until midnight or later.

Once we had to get some outdoor scenes at dawn. I had to climb a flight of stairs up the side of a block of London tenements. I was climbing those stairs every single dawn for eight weeks.

I never saw the finished film until a year afterwards, when I was in Dublin and it was showing. When it came to that scene the sight of those stairs so exhausted me that I felt I'd done the whole thing over once more, and when I got up to leave I found my knees were so weak that I had to sit down again.

It was at this stage in my career that Archie and I decided to part. I knew I would be happier on my own, and not continually ruled and dominated by him. I knew, too, that if I did not find the courage to break the habit of obeying him which I had grown up with ever since I was sixteen, I should never be able to make a full and happy life for myself as I grew older.

The decision, and the break, were not made easy for me, but this time I knew that to give in, and go back, would be fatal. I left "The Towers" with all its ostentation and unhappy memories, for ever.

Some years later our marriage was dissolved and Archie eventually married Annie Lipman.

Meanwhile I had to find somewhere to live and I wanted somewhere as different from "The Towers" as it was possible to find. The one place in London which had seemed like a home to me after Mum and Dad had moved to Peacehaven, had been John and Henry's studio. Now I decided that a studio would be just right for me, and I found one, near theirs, up a back lane in St. John's Wood.

The studio itself which was built on to the back of an old-fashioned four-storey house, looked like a good storage place for potatoes. It had a stone floor, and a little alcove where there was a bath and a cooker; when you didn't need the bath you could cover it over with boards and use it as a table. Upstairs there was one tiny attic and Auntie Mar-

garet, who was living with me, and I shared this as a bedroom.

To get to the place you had to go through an unlit
alleyway by the side of the house and Archie's brother,
Bert Aza, who was still my manager and my dearest friend,
was horrified with the whole set-up when he saw it.

Though he never insisted upon the same magnificence
that Archie had liked, and though he understood the pleasure I got from sprucing up my "potato store" and making
it into a home, even he couldn't accept this one.

"Live where you like, Grace," he said. "Only for goodness sake do choose somewhere where you don't have to go
sneaking up dark alleys at two o'clock in the morning when
you get home from late night shows. It worries me to death.
Anyone could hit you over the head and we shouldn't
know for hours. Besides, you can't ask anyone there. What
would people say if they knew the famous Gracie Fields
was living in a garret with a stone floor?"

But I bought a lovely carpet, and a Bechstein piano for
my "garret" and loved the place, stone floor and all. It was
adequate, comfortable, and I was at ease there. I suppose it
was my own personal stepping stone towards living my own
life.

I could lunch at the Ritz, sing at the Palladium, sign a
thousand autographs a day, meet the important people who
always seemed to crop up, but when I got back to the
studio and Auntie Margaret's welcoming smile it felt like
a real home.

Though I was called famous, earned about six hundred
pounds a week outside of films, and had to behave like a
"personality," in my own private life I was still learning to
grow up, and my studio gave me all the pleasure and thrill
that most girls get at eighteen from their first "Bed-sitter"

when they leave home for the first time and can do exactly as they please.

And then, just when I had my first small home in London, I got a letter from Capri, from young Ettore Patrizi. His father's house, the one I had stayed in in Capri, was for sale, at fifteen thousand pounds.

After that I didn't have a moment's peace. I couldn't bear the thought of anyone else owning that house in that beautiful bay, yet I didn't know whether I could buy it myself: fifteen thousand pounds seemed an awful lot of money and I didn't have that much. I just didn't know how much money I really made, had, or spent.

I sang the songs and made the films and all the bills had gone in to Archie and Bert who handled all the money.

"What am I going to do?" I asked John Flanagan.

First of all he suggested sending an architect to Capri to value the house. I got about twenty excited cables from Capri from this architect, a lot of travelling bills, and never saw or heard from him again. But his last cable had told me that they would now accept eleven thousand pounds for the property.

Then we found an English lawyer who got in touch with an Italian one. He went to Capri and cabled that the property was not worth even six thousand pounds. They were selling the house before it fell down, the land was uncultivated, and most of it was rock with no vegetation. "Obviously you would be mad to buy it," said my London lawyer blinking at me over his spectacles.

"I know it sounds daft," I explained earnestly, "but I want it for when I retire. I'll be old when I'm fifty, and you see, I'm always thinking of retiring."

Since I was thirty-two at the time this convinced him I was mad, and he would have nothing further to do with my crazy venture.

I plagued everyone to put me in touch with someone who knew something about Italian property, and finally got an introduction to the legal adviser to the British Embassy in Rome. By this time I was in a real muddle over all the various prices, first fifteen thousand pounds, then eleven thousand pounds, then six thousand pounds. I didn't know what it was all about. He understood it all much better than I. "The first thing you must do is *not* to tell a soul you want it," he said.

"But I want it more than anything in the world!" "Yes," he said patiently, "but you mustn't *say* so. It will have to be sold by auction."

A year later I was in Rochdale giving a charity concert and staying with my mother's old friend, Bertha Schofield, who now kept an off-licence there. A telegram came, and it was from the legal adviser. I owned the whole of the Patrizi property, shack, broken-down yard, an entire uncultivated hillside and a long rocky beach.

I sat down at Bertha's kitchen-table, wrote out the cheque, walked to the pillar box and posted it before I could change my mind. Then I went back to Bertha's kitchen. "I've bought a piece of ground, in Capri, with a house on it," I said, "and I've only got twenty-five pounds left in the bank."

Bertha sat down heavily. "A house in a foreign country," she said. "Over with all them I-talians! Tha' must be 'oop t'pole, Grace," and then with a sharp glance at me, "does your Mumma know?"

I shook my head. "Ee," said Bertha who remembered the old days, "tha's best be careful how tha' tells her or she'll give thee a reet good clout!"

"Do you think I'll be able to keep it?" I asked her anxiously, running up the scale to a top note. "With twenty-five pounds in t'bank?" asked Bertha.

"I'll have to go over there and take a look at it, I've never even *seen* the whole place properly yet."

Bertha got up and put a kettle on. "Have a cup of tea," she advised. "If tha' doesn't need one, ah do. Ee, luv, tha's got some pluck."

I started walking round clearing my throat nervously, then I let out a couple of good piercing notes that shook her little kitchen. I felt better after I'd heard them. "It's still there, luv," I said. "I can sing for a few more pounds yet."

"Tha'll need to," said Bertha drily.

Neither she nor I dreamed that the "few" pounds would, in fact, be half a million pounds from films alone, in the next five years, but even while we were talking the phone rang and Bert Aza asked me to come straight back to London. "I've got a film offer here for you for seventy-two thousand pounds," he said.

The offer was for six films over six years at twelve thousand pounds a film, but it tied me to Archie Pitt for those six years, and, much as I needed the money then, I could see that even though we were no longer living as husband and wife I would still have to obey Archie, still try to conform to his standards as "his film star." But to turn down seventy-two thousand pounds just because I wanted my own sort of freedom seemed like lunacy. Well, so did buying a property in Capri seem like lunacy, yet I was happier now than I'd been for years.

As usual I took the problem to John Flanagan and Henry Savage. They were admiring a china shepherdess figurine that John had just bought in the Caledonian market.

"Look at this contract, John," I said. "It's for seventy-two thousand pounds, but it's for six years, and Archie wants me to sign."

John didn't even turn round. Instead he held out the

figurine. "Look at this beautiful little creature; she cost me only four shillings." That was all he said.

I stood very still in the shabby studio and looked at John's absorbed face, at the fluted folds of the little shepherdess's dress so beautifully created out of china: then I thought of my ramshackle property in Capri, and I learned the last and most valuable lesson that John and Henry could teach me.

A few shillings could buy happiness for them, but seventy-two thousand pounds was going to buy me nothing but misery and the inability to enjoy what I had.

I went back to Bert Aza. "Tell Archie I won't sign with him, Bert. No hard feelings, but I can't live that sort of life for the next six years. Get me another film offer because I need *some* brass, but I don't care how little it is."

Bert, and his wife Lillian, who was to become one of my dearest friends, looked at me in silence. Then Bert put out his hand. "It's okay, Grace," he said. "I'll look around." One week later he phoned me. "Grace," he said excitedly, "R.K.O. will give you twenty thousand pounds for just one film."

I made the film, *One Week of Grace*, and it was just as much of an ordeal as the others had been, but this time I took my snapshot album of all my pictures of Capri to look at, in between takes, and that made it bearable. Whenever I thought I couldn't stand the studio for another minute I'd tell myself, "Making films is the price you pay for Capri," and that way I got it done. But, when it was finished I told Bert "We'll never sign for another film, Bert, never. I'm really only happy on the stage, so turn all film offers down."

This decision, for some reason I shall never understand, seemed to send the British film makers crazy. "They're offering you twenty-five thousand pounds a film now." Bert told me in a few days' time.

"Refuse it, Bert."

The phone rang again. Bert's voice was a thin wail. "They're offering thirty thousand pounds." I gulped. "Thirty thousand! But that's ridiculous."

"Grace, it may be ridiculous," said Bert plaintively, "but you may never get the chance again."

When you've been poor as long as we had those words make sense, and it seemed downright wicked to turn work and money away.

"Oh, all right," I said, "tell 'em I'll do it."

I made two more films between vaudeville appearances and recordings. "Now that's the lot, Bert."

Bert nodded. "I know how you feel, Grace. If anybody else asks, I'll tell them you wouldn't make another film for less than forty thousand pounds!"

We both chuckled and stirred our tea in the old white cups that we'd been using in Bert's office for the past five years. "That'll fix 'em, Bert, sure enough."

I packed my bag and went to Peacehaven for a few days' rest. I'd scarcely had time to change into my old gardening trousers when taxi brakes squealed outside my high wall. It was Bert looking as though he didn't know whether to laugh or to cry.

"I told them you wanted forty thousand pounds a picture, Grace," he said. His round face was comic with dismay. "They're offering you a contract at forty thousand pounds a picture, but not just for one, but for four!"

I sat down hard on the front step. "Now I know they're all barmy," I said.

And it was at this time, when the crazy years were really beginning, that I met Monty Banks. I was thirty-eight.

It's funny, when you look back, how little you realise

what a casual meeting can do to change the whole course
of your life.

My introduction to Monty was just such a meeting.

I dreaded film making but Monty was already renowned
for his skill at handling comedy pictures, and my sister
Betty, who had made a film with him, assured me that
once I was directed by him I would even *enjoy* filming.
"He's a brilliant director, Grace," she assured me.

When I first saw this short little Italian with curly black
hair, overdressed in a too-perfectly pressed suit and a silk
shirt, I wanted to giggle.

He came down to Peacehaven for Sunday lunch, and I
was put out, because Sundays with the family were about
the only times I ever got to myself. I wasn't going to
smarten up just for him so he found me in my old trousers,
filthy from playing in the garden with kids and the dogs,
and with my hair all screwed up because I'd just washed
it.

When we met we just stared at each other.

Years later Monty told me of that meeting. "I'd just
read a newspaper article about you, calling you the richest
working girl in the world. I'd been so careful to look my
best when I met you, and when I saw you I couldn't believe my eyes."

By that time too I knew that Monty would have taken
hours to get ready to meet me. He'd come from the same
poor beginnings as I had, and when he was nervous at
meeting someone important he spent hours dressing himself up. This was his way of bolstering his self-confidence,
it was his war-paint.

But then, on that first Sunday, I had no idea that Monty
was going to take over my life where Archie had left off,
though, in his own fashion, he did.

It was a very different fashion from Archie's, yet our

98

lives together were built from the same sort of partnership of work and understanding.

He would strut and show off with the movie magnates, loved to be photographed with gorgeous girls, but he also loved to come home, put on an apron, and cook. He loved cooking.

he liked simple things like her

I suppose it was this contrast in his nature that made him fit so easily into our crazy household, because it *was* crazy just then. The time had come when all that money was hitting *me* right between the eyes. From worrying over only twenty-five pounds left in the bank, I now seemed to have thousands.

So we had my parents, Mum and Dad, living in ever-spreading glory at Peacehaven, and no sooner had Monty learned his way around that home than Dad started telling him about the one in Capri.

"'Ave you seen our Grace's place over there?" he demanded.

Monty shook his head. Dad grunted and Mum folded her hands primly. "It's very nice," she said stoutly.

"Nice!" roared Dad, launching into the tale. "First of all she goes and buys half a blasted mountain, then she carts me over there to see that it gets knocked down.

"You can't make them I-talians understand Lancashire, you know," he continued to Italian-born Monty. "Forty of 'em she had working out there all summer. I give 'em a job to do, and when I turn round they've all gone fishing, or swimming, or drinking that vino. I had to lug all them stones about myself, put new windows in the place, and build a path to get to it . . . crazy blasted place. . . ." He paused and then looked sorrowfully at Monty. "All t'summer I were there," he said again, "and not one good mug of beer in the whole place."

Mum frowned impatiently, but had to add her bit. "I

must say I don't like that Vesuvius being so near," she said. "Everything looks like it's crumbling down to me. But I did teach the woman over there how to make good Yorkshire pudding, and happen it won't be so bad when we go over again."

"When you get there," sister Betty chimed in, "you have to drive to Grace's place in carriages. Honestly, Monty, with me mumma and dad stuck up there in front, and all of us following along behind in pairs, we look like a ruddy Roman chariot race."

Edith completed the picture of my Capri paradise for Monty. "I said to our Grace when I got there," she said wistfully, " 'why on earth couldn't you have picked somewhere really nice, nearer home, like Bournemouth or Southport'."

Much later Monty came to see me on business with Bert Aza at my home in London. At least he was spared the St. John's Wood Studio. By this time Bert had persuaded me to buy what he called a decent house. I'd got one in Finchley Road, called "Greentrees," and I'd got my own little household together there with Auntie Margaret, and a fan of mine called Mary Barratt. — *does she have notes?*

Mary Barratt had once written me a letter which contained so much helpful and amusing comment on my work that I'd replied to it. She wrote back again and asked if, when I was appearing in the North, she could come backstage and meet me.

She came when I was in Blackpool. I found she was working as a companion to a woman living in the area. Something about her appealed to me enormously, and I'd found myself saying: "Would you like to come and work for me?"

Her reply settled it. Since she was a fan of mine obviously there was nothing she would have liked more, but she'd answered: "I'd love to, if you can wait for me. I can't leave the woman I'm working for until I'm sure she'll be all right."

That's the sort of loyalty I admire in folks. I was ready to wait for Mary and I've always been glad I did. From that time on she became my companion and helpmate.

So now the three of us, Auntie Margaret, still as Lancashire as ever, Mary, and I were installed in "Greentrees" with a constant company of composers, pianists and music publishers. We made as unlikely a household as you'd find anywhere, with an Irish gardener, Seamus, and my Italian maid, Flo Flo.

There was this fine big house, furnished like a palace. On my own I think I'd gone even one better than Archie because this time I'd left everything to the professional decorators before I moved in, and *their* idea of a home for "the richest working girl in the world" was to give me a Hollywood "set" for a drawing room.

It had a yellow fitted carpet. The walls were white, the grand piano was white, all the furniture was white, and so was the silk brocade upholstery with gold threads in it.

The huge curtains were of pink silk damask and the great chandeliers cost a fortune.

It looked so sugar-and-spicey we never sat in the place for fear of mucking it up.

But I soon got tired of this. For one thing, one piano wasn't enough. Mary and Auntie Margaret were half scared to let all these composer chaps go into the white and gold tomb if I wasn't there, so I had to buy another grand piano which we shoved in the dining-room—then we couldn't eat for music.

We bought a third, and put it in the library . . . no one had much time for reading anyway. Finally we got a fourth and there was nowhere for that to go except in my bedroom, so it went there.

There was always some fellow trying out his latest tune on every piano in the house. None of them ever seemed to have pianos—or homes—of their own.

"I've had enough of this," I said one day. "There's that great big fancy room going to waste with no one in it. Move the billiard table down there, serve meals in there, put a bar in, and let 'em get on with it!"

Mary did that, with many—justified—misgivings for my yellow carpet and my beautiful white furniture. After that nobody seemed to go home at all and the music went on all night till I found that poor Auntie Margaret wasn't getting any sleep.

"We'll have to start a curfew," I said to Mary. "Tell 'em all they've *all* got to buzz off after two o'clock, no matter what."

Now I was being rich in my own way, and it didn't seem so bad, though, in a way, all the big money I was earning worried me.

When I had worked a week, and got a week's wages, I could enjoy spending it. Every pound was precious, and belonged to me.

When I had earned one hundred pounds a week I felt wonderfully important and successful. I could buy presents, I could spend five pounds and think: "Well, there's ninety-five pounds left over till next week."

But the big money I was earning now seemed unreal. Songs I had made into gramophone discs months before, and long forgotten, were still pouring money into the bank. Every mail brought offers, as well as begging letters.

Sometimes I felt as though my mother had touched Aladdin's lamp when she had said: "We're going 'oop." It seemed we couldn't stop going up, and above all things I was determined that every one of my family was going along with me. But I didn't quite know how to go about it.

It was easy with Mum and Dad. If I'd still been a mill girl in Rochdale it would have been right and natural that a good bit of my wages should have gone to them as they got older. They accepted this as much as I did. But with my sisters Betty and Edith, who were both married, and with my brother Tommy, it was more difficult.

Every now and then I still went through agonies of doubt and loneliness that no matter how I tried to keep us all together as we used to be, all the fame, and all the money, would make us drift apart.

If I tried to give too many presents to Edith I might hurt her husband's feelings. If I tried to give too many presents to Betty her red-headed pride would rear up. And something warned me that if I gave too much to young Tommy who was rapidly making a name for himself, I might undermine his self-confidence and determination to make good in his own right.

While I was making my first film with Monty, *Queen of Hearts*, I was playing at the Holborn Empire every night, in vaudeville. I was working like a fool for radio, stage, gramophone recordings, films, and the money seemed to be flowing in.

I was always tired, but there was always something to do, somebody who wanted me, for a charity show, to open this, lay the foundation stone for that, for more work, and still more work.

I remember sitting in my dressing-room between shows feeling muddled and miserable again.

It seemed so long since Betty had called me up, since Edith had been round to see me. I longed to see them because, for weeks, I'd been hatching my own plot to make them feel that what happened to one of the Stansfields happened to all of the Stansfields . . . not just Grace.

I'd just written out three cheques, one for Betty, one for Edith, and one for Tommy, for ten thousand pounds each, and I was going to give them as sort of special Christmas presents.

That way, it seemed to me, it would be their money, *family* money, not mine, and they needn't keep thanking me when I didn't want to be thanked, or feeling embarrassed at too many presents.

I was sitting there, wondering how I'd pluck up courage to tell them what I'd done, and to explain how I felt, and why, when the door opened and Edith came in.

It was so rare for Edith to come to the theatre that it was like an answer to all the doubts I'd been having. "Edith!" I said. "Oh, luv, it's so good to see you . . ." but she cut me short.

Edith was always the gentle one of the family, but now she stood there, her small face angry, her shoulders very square, and slammed the dressing-room door behind her.

"I've just come, Grace, to tell you what I think," she stormed, "Betty isn't well, and you know that none of us can possibly have the good times that you get . . ."

"But, Edith," I began, "that's just what . . ."

"Here you are earning all this money, the great Gracie Fields, on the stage, on the wireless, on the films, and what time have you got for your own sister?"

"Edie," I begged, the tears streaming down my face. "Edie, look, I've just . . ."

"The least you could have done would have been to send our Betty some flowers, and a hundred pounds or something, but you're always too busy now, too much darned work to . . ."

"Edie, I'm trying to tell . . ."

"I don't care for myself," Edith rushed on, refusing to be interrupted, "but if you haven't got the decency to think about your family . . ."

There was a loud bang on the door. "On stage, Miss Fields," yelled the call boy.

I grabbed a towel, dabbed my eyes, and croaked at Edith "For goodness sake, wait!"

Then I flew down the stairs to the stage. I was doing cod-opera. I wondered as I hurried to the wings if tonight would be the first night when my tears would get the better of me, and I'd not be able to sound one note.

But I'd had to do this before. Out there you had to make them laugh with no heed for your own feelings. I made them laugh. Then I rushed back to the dressing-room. Edie was still there. Before she could open her mouth I grabbed the cheque book which was still lying on my dressing table among the clutter of make-up jars and sticks. "Look Edie, *please* look," I said desperately. "I'd written them before you came in. I've been that bothered, wondering how to do it for ages."

Edith looked down at the three cheques made out to herself, and Betty and Tommy.

Still before she could say anything I went on, "I know I'm a few days early, but . . ." and I faltered, ". . . only I didn't know how to give them to you, luv. I thought as it was Christmas you'd accept it that way.

"All this brass is no good to me unless we're all sharing it, and I miss you all so much."

And then Edith and I sat there like a couple of fools, crying, and laughing and hugging each other. "Oh," I said, "if only I could explain to you all. Without my family I'm no good, I'm not myself, and I don't know what to do."

Perhaps the best way I can describe my warm, lovely family is to tell their answer to my Christmas gift that year. All three of them told me: "We don't need that much, so we're not going to spend it. We're going to invest it. You never know in this business when you might go broke. If anything should ever happen to you, luv, you know that the three of us can look after you."

So, all round, it couldn't have been more all right.

"Eh, I'm glad I've got that off me chest," I said. "Now I can get on with some of the other things I want to do." So I took care of some of the charities I specially wanted to help, and we enlarged the orphanage. I bought cars, got all my groceries at Fortnum and Mason, kept an open house, and just didn't know how much I owned, or, as I was to find out soon enough, how much I owed—to the tax men.

All I knew was that I was getting very tired, and that I wanted more time to spend with my family.

"After this lot we'll have to stop making films," I told Bert and Monty. "All this is sending me silly. I don't want to make any more films, not even if they offer fifty thousand pounds each."

That's when Hollywood sent for me, to do four films, *at* fifty thousand pounds each! And it was about this time that the Income Tax folk started to send me in demands for many thousands of pounds.

I just hadn't realised that I ought to have saved at least half of all the money I earned to meet this tax, though Bert had warned me and tried to explain it to me often enough. Now I understood all too clearly. By the time the tax people had sent in all their bills Monty reckoned I'd have to sell my big house "Greentrees," and all its trimmings to help pay some of the debts I owed to the Inland Revenue.

"I can't sell it," I protested. "I've just got it all in order."

"You'll have to sell it," said Monty. "And all the things that are in it."

"No!"

"Yes! And at once." *—tax problems*

I had to sell at a loss because I needed the money straight away, the Inland Revenue weren't in the mood to wait.

"I always knew everything was barmy," I said, "but they're not going to have my goldfish, or my tiger lilies in the garden. I planted them myself, they're *mine*."

So, in the dead of night, I went back to "Greentrees" and scooped out every goldfish in the pond and dug up all my tiger lilies.

Then I tried out my voice. It still sounded like a steam whistle. I reckoned I could get through those four films at fifty thousand all right, and still keep Capri, which was the only home that really mattered to me. At least the Income Tax couldn't take that.

5

EVEN though Betty had promised me I would enjoy film-making with Monty, and though I liked Monty very much, my anxiety had not been lessened by the fact that unless *Queen of Hearts* was finished on time it would upset all the arrangements made for me to do a tour of South Africa.

In my experience the constant bungling and delays meant that a film *never* finished on time. If this one was late it would mean that either the picture, or the big variety show I was taking to South Africa, would end in disaster. Either way an awful lot of money and other people's jobs were at stake.

On the first day of shooting I arrived as usual at seven A.M. and Monty was already there, surrounded by technicians, continuity girls, extras and small part players. They were all drinking tea and shaking with laughter.

"Hallo," I said. "What's the joke at this hour of the morning?"

Monty spun round. He was still chuckling, but he seemed surprised.

"What are you doing here?" he asked. "We won't need you for two days, you're not in this first scene. Didn't you know?"

"Yes, I knew, but before I've always been wanted on the set whether I was in the scene or not. Still, now I'm here I'd like to stay for a bit, if you don't mind." I wanted to watch Monty Banks work anyway.

"Then pray be seated!" he said with a grin and waved me to my canvas chair with an elaborate bow. A few seconds later I leapt out of it with a shriek. He'd lit a bonfire of newspapers under me. That was my first experience of Monty's practical jokes, he played them all the time, on anyone, and anywhere.

We were still laughing at my bonfire as Monty bustled people into position for the first scene and the lights went on.

He got started at once. The players, still half smiling, were giving an easy relaxed performance. Always before I had watched the small part players move on to the set wary and frozen with apprehension to do their comedy roles. When, before she became a star, Vivien Leigh played a small part in *Look Up and Laugh* she was so nervous of the director that several times I found her nearly in tears. In contrast Monty, by his deliberate clowning, got everybody all unbuttoned and easy. He kept them that way. He seemed so confident and to know exactly what he was trying to do and how best to achieve it.

I sat fascinated all morning, watching.

Two days later I turned up at the studios for my own work and found everybody there except Monty.

"Where is he?" I asked. His assistant director grinned. "You watch him, Miss Fields. He's always exactly twenty minutes late. He comes rushing in and chases that twenty minutes for the rest of the day! That's how he always manages to finish his films ahead of time."

This was good news for me, and sure enough, punctually twenty minutes "late," in came Monty. "Sorry I'm late,

folks! Come on, then, let's get started—gotta catch up!"
An instant later he had us all laughing at some absurdity.

His feel for comedy was instinctive and I learnt this in
the first scene I played for him. When we reached the end
of it there was no call for "Cut!" so I just kept going, ad-
libbing to keep up the sense of the scene and wondering
why Monty wasn't calling a halt.

We seemed to go on like this all the morning while
Monty just sat there, watching, and lighting one cigarette
after another. Sometimes I hesitated or dried up, but he
would wave his hand impatiently and I plunged on again.

Towards the end of the day I was getting worried. I
thought perhaps he was getting so tired of my brand of
comedy that he just couldn't begin the wearying job of
putting me right every time. In the end I went up to him
and said: "Look, Monty, if you don't like what I'm doing,
please tell me, and I'll try to do it as you want, but it's
getting me bothered just going on and on and on and you
never shouting 'cut'."

He roared with laughter and gave my arm a reassuring
squeeze. "You keep going just as you are," he said. "That
stuff you're doing naturally at the end of each scene are
the only parts I'm keeping in the film so far!"

They were, too. He invited me to see the rushes with
him that evening. Then I saw that the unrehearsed parts
looked far livelier, much funnier than the set lines from the
script, and I saw where Monty's skill as a director came in.

He used to go through all the day's takes when we had
finished, and get them edited, and often he was at the
studio till two or three A.M. But no matter how far past
midnight he worked he'd always be on the set first thing
next morning, punctually twenty minutes late.

We got through that film so quickly and happily that we

were well ahead of schedule, and I had no worries about my sailing date for South Africa.

And then, right in the last week, one of the actors was ill and we reached the final day with still a lot to do. I was due to get the boat-train early the following day and there was poor Monty with nearly a week's work to complete in about twelve hours.

There was a lot of the usual good-humoured larking about and he encouraged it, as he always did. No one seemed to realise the urgency of it all except Monty and me, and, during the mid-day break, some of the boys and girls chose that moment, of all times, to celebrate someone's birthday. They came back in the kind of giggling mood that doesn't seem to realise when play stops and real work begins.

I felt sorry for Monty. For nearly two months he had worked eighteen hours a day on the film, living on cups of coffee and endless cigarettes, tireless, cheerful, and always encouraging. Now here he was, on this last day, with most of his players and technical staff in a mood of clowning and still so much to do.

Yet, without once losing his temper or with any heavy show of authority, he got through the picture, on time.

It was well after midnight when we finished and some of the people who had been most boisterous were now feeling sorry for themselves. Monty was pale with fatigue. He was so dazed with tiredness that he didn't see a piece of scenery in his way. He walked straight into it and injured his eyes.

In the slap-happy atmosphere of the last day everyone roared with laughter and made the usual jokes about black eyes. Monty took it all in good part and grinned back, tired and hurt as he was. No one seemed at all concerned that he might have done serious damage to his eyes. It suddenly struck me that I knew nothing at all about his home background and I wondered if there would be anyone waiting for him when he got to his home, and whether he knew where to get a doctor.

I didn't have much time myself to get home, collect my luggage and get the boat-train, but I asked one of the people in the studio if they knew where Monty lived, and if there was someone there.

I vaguely knew that he had been married, and divorced, from a wife who had been mentally disturbed, and that, in some way, he still looked after her, but other than that I didn't know much about his personal life at all.

Someone told me casually that they thought his sister from Italy was living with him, but she didn't speak any English.

I glanced at Monty and saw that his eyes were swelling rapidly and that he was in considerable pain. I kept thinking of him as I drove home, and decided that something had better be done about that injury, I didn't like the look of it.

It was terribly late but I knew someone who could help. I got on the phone to Lottie Albert at our orphanage and said, "That eye specialist who's done all the work for our kiddies, Lottie, Mr. Rycroft, do you think you could get hold of him? Wake him up, and ask him if he'll go round to this address." I gave her Monty's. "Tell him there's a chap there with a badly hurt eye who needs looking after."

Lottie promised to see to it and I could rely on Lottie. She ran the orphanage wonderfully, and if she promised to do something it was as good as done. I felt easier in my mind about Monty's eyes and rushed on to get the boat-train.

Before we sailed I had a phone call from Mr. Rycroft. "Just in case you were worried about your friend," he said, "it will be all right now, but it was a good thing you sent me round at once, you certainly saved the vision of at least one of his eyes! That was a very nasty wound he had there."

He added: "I had to fix him up without being able to ease the pain for him and he never murmured. Remarkable chap. What is he, Italian?"

"He's just like one of us, a hard working lad who's got on in the world a bit," I said, as I thanked Mr. Rycroft.

I was very pleased I'd been able to do something for Monty and sailed to South Africa feeling that if I had to make more films with him it wouldn't be quite such an ordeal, he was a nice little chap and he certainly knew his job.

I tried to rest on the voyage out. I was terribly tired and run down and I expected the South African tour to be a challenge. They had never seen me before, except on the movies, and I thought I'd have to work pretty hard to get myself established as a variety star there. In a way I was looking forward to it, I liked a fight to win an audience. But it wasn't like that at all.

I was totally unprepared for my reception in South Africa, and when I left the ship the welcome there un-nerved me.

The quayside was packed with thousands of people blowing hooters, throwing confetti, paper streamers and flowers. They carried banners "WELCOME GRACIE FIELDS," and we had to ride in an open car through streets so thronged you might have thought it was the King.

I hope it won't sound conceited if I say that, on that South African tour, I think I began to realise something of the tremendous emotional and physical strain our Royal family must stand up to, whenever thousands of people constantly demonstrate affection for them.

I once heard someone comment on the composure of our young Queen throughout the tumultuous welcomes of her Coronation tour: "You'd think it would move her to tears."

In my own small way I've learned that once you let such tremendous receptions move you to tears, you're done. There comes a point when you just have to weld your heart and mind and feelings into a sort of shock-absorber so that, as wave after wave of emotion rolls towards you, you have the strength to take it, to smile, to control your voice, and to speak.

Afterwards, and especially if you're alone, you feel wrung out, shaken, and often frightened. You have an impossible need to run back to all those wonderful people and start trying to explain: "Look, I'm just an ordinary person, there's nothing about me that deserves all this, please understand. . . ."

But you can't. And to be given this sort of acclaim is one of the most humbling experiences I know.

For my first show out there I did a thirty minute act which I thought far too long. Next morning the papers indicated it had been far too short! It seemed the audience had expected to hear every song I'd ever sung, in films, or on records.

But all the criticism, instead of being directed at me, was somehow thrust on to the orchestra!

It just shows you the advantage of having a reputation. If the show was a flop it couldn't be Gracie Fields—it must be the miserable, anonymous orchestra.

I wrote to the newspapers and told them the truth. I had been nervous after my tremendous welcome; I had no idea they expected a longer show; the fault was all mine and had nothing to *do* with the orchestra. I promised if the critics would come and give me a second chance—at my expense—I would try to do better. Generously they did come, and all was well.

Afterwards the orchestra stood up and gave me a private cheer of their own, and, when I left Capetown, they presented me with a silver plaque, and I'm told that nobody in show business has ever had that happen to them.

I am very proud of that plaque: "To Our Gracie from the orchestra" it says, and it hangs in my living-room in Capri today.

And then, all the way from Capetown to Johannesburg, the crowds started pouring down to the railway tracks and besieging the train. At the first stop when I saw them, I said to my brother Tommy; "C'mon, let's go and see what's happening." We joined the great throng and asked what it was all about. *I was also there*

"We're waiting to see Gracie Fields, she's on this train." Tommy and I stared at each other. Suddenly I realised what they'd said. "Crumbs!" I said to Tommy. "That's me!" and I had to run back to the train before they recognised me. They wouldn't leave until I came out on the observation platform at the rear of the coaches and sang. This happened at every station and whistle-stop for the whole of that long journey. I shall never forget it.

That tour could never have been such a success without the brilliance of my pianist, Harry Parr-Davies, who wrote so many of the numbers I've sung and recorded. By the time we went to South Africa I'd known Harry for four years.

He'd walked into my dressing-room one day, a long lanky lad of seventeen, looking half scared. This was the time when song writers were always pursuing me, making me listen to dozens of tunes a day. We'd had to give orders that no more could come to see me, for I never got a moment's peace.

Harry had got past the stage door-keeper because he was so young he looked like a messenger boy.

When he reached my room someone said sharply: "What do you want?" When he mumbled something about a song he looked so nervous I hadn't the heart to turn him out.

There was a piano in my dressing-room. "Well go on, son, play your tune while I'm dressing," I'd told him. I went behind a screen to get into my costume. I had to go on-stage in a few minutes and knew he couldn't keep me.

But the tune surprised me. It was very good, and I told him so. "Go away and finish it, I can use it." He blushed miserably, then stammered: "I can't, I haven't got a piano." I laughed. "All right," I said, "you can use mine."

The number went into my next film. After that Harry had songs in nearly every one of my films. He wrote "Pedro The Fisherman," "Wish Me Luck," "Sing As We Go" and many other big hits.

At that time I always had my stage set as a drawing-room, with a grand piano, which was never played.

One night, as Harry stood in the wings with me before I went on I said: "That piano looks proper lonely out there Harry, why don't you go and sit at it?" He had never been on a stage before and he was terrified. But I got him at the piano that night, and he played for me for the next nine years.

I fool about with my voice so much that dozens of professional accompanists have told me, "You don't need a pianist, you need a mind-reader!"

Well, with Harry, I'd found one. No matter what key I chose to lark about in, what phrasing or timing I'd decide to do, Harry always seemed to know.

We became firm friends. He was as Welsh as they come, and temperamental, and would often pick a row just to make himself feel better. But we had a brother-and-sister

116

affection for each other and he became a part of the family, who accepted him as much as I did.

When we all went down to Peacehaven for week-ends everyone took it for granted that Harry would spend most of his time at the piano playing like an angel, and shouting like a devil for his breakfast right up till tea-time.

He'd get at the piano as soon as he was up, and yell for his breakfast. It would be brought to him, on a tray, and put on top of the piano. He'd let it get cold. Then he'd shout. Another breakfast would be brought in. He'd let that get cold and create again. One Sunday Mary Barratt and my mother brought him no less than seven trays of breakfast, and, in the middle of the afternoon, he was still carrying on that he hadn't had a hot cup of tea since he'd got up!

"Pour the next lot over his head," I suggested, amiably.

"No," they said, "we don't mind how many trays we take in, or how much he shouts, just so long as he keeps on playing."

When war was declared Harry was conscripted. His songs had already made him a respectable fortune even though he was then only in his twenties. Although he was in uniform he was "posted" by the authorities to be my pianist at the war concerts I gave at the Albert Hall.

This suited Private Harry Parr-Davies very well. He booked a suite at the Dorchester and bribed a Corporal of the Guards to clean his boots and buttons. He was the smartest private soldier in London for weeks until his Commanding Officer found out!

When he was with me in South Africa the funniest thing I remember about him then was his constant bickering with the conductor in Capetown.

Harry came from Neath, near Swansea and had a pronounced Welsh accent. So did the conductor of the orchestra. When they spoke to each other, Harry thought the conductor was constantly taking him off. The conductor thought the same of Harry. Their final quarrel . . . "I'll speak as I like . . ." . . . "and so will I! . . ." both in the strongest Welsh which neither of them could help, had to be heard to be believed.

He was only twenty-one then and it is tragic to think that some one with so much talent, and so much to live for, should have died when he was only forty. —why?

When I returned to England I had only a few weeks there before going to Hollywood for more films, and I was to make some of them with Monty Banks.

If I had not grown to *enjoy* making films with Monty exactly, at least, I didn't dread them so much. I felt safe with him. He was a skilled and experienced director and I'm sure I should never have survived in Hollywood without his help and guidance. I wasn't up to all the tricks of the trade, but Monty was.

I remember how Constance Bennett, in a film I did with her, held up everything until the scene was re-set to show her best profile. She caught my eye and said: "If you think I'm holding it up you should make a picture with Claudette Colbert—and that's why she *is* Claudette Colbert!"

It had been the same with Victor McLaglen who starred with me in *We're Going to be Rich*.

I liked Victor, but he had been brought up in a hard school. He kept moving slowly around me during dialogue so that, to keep my face towards him, I had practically to turn my back to the cameras. I was thinking of my lines and paid no heed to whether I was being made to say them over my shoulder or not.

But Victor would forget his lines, or give me a wrong cue whenever I, and not he, was facing the camera. I didn't realise this, and couldn't think what was going wrong. Monty could. He stopped the cameras.

"Look, Victor," he'd say, quietly, "we'll keep taking this scene until you're both helping each other. Grace will stand it as long as you can, and I shall stand it longer than either of you. Now, let's take a rest."

A few minutes later, as we rested, all rather tense, Monty began clowning. He was a great clown and could always break up an atmosphere by his antics. He'd put on a slapstick act that made us all laugh, then he'd take us back to work. Things always went smoothly then, and they always went the way Monty wanted them to. I was glad he would be waiting for me when I got to America.

I was told that the big chief of Twentieth-Century Fox, who was paying the two hundred thousand pounds for four films, or, as they put it, "the highest salary ever paid to a human being," was Mr. Darryl Zanuck. But the man with whom I had signed the contract in London was Mr. Joe Schenck.

When my boat docked in New York Monty was there to meet me, and to tell me that Twentieth-Century Fox had prepared a banquet for America's two hundred most important columnists to meet me, and that many of them were already on the dockside.

"Whatever you do, mention Darryl Zanuck," Monty kept saying anxiously.

"Who's he?" I asked. Monty nearly died.

"I'll mention Mr. Schenck," I said.

"No," shouted Monty, "Darryl Zanuck."

"I *can't*, Monty. I don't know him. It's Mr. Schenck."

"It's Darryl Zanuck!"

"NO, Monty, it's Joe Schenck."

After Monty had nearly gone crazy over this, he then nearly died for a second time when he took in my appearance.

"My God, you look a mess, Grace! This is America! . . . look at your make-up! Look at your hair!"

I patted my hair, it looked all right to me, I'd done it myself. But I said obediently, "All right, Monty, you know America better than I do; take me to the right kind of hairdresser."

He whisked me off to the posh Ambassador's hotel in New York and brought the chief hairdresser to my suite. "The smartest hair-do you can give her," he commanded. Then he disappeared.

When the girl finished with my hair I looked in the mirror. I'd never seen anything like it. It looked like a Japanese pagoda!

"What've you done, luv?" I asked her faintly. She glanced at me pityingly: "It's the latest style," she said, as though she was teaching a two-year-old.

Harry Parr-Davies who was in my sitting-room nodded. "Looks very smart, Grace," he said absently, and returned to his magazine.

Well, whenever I thought something was real daft I was frequently wrong. I thought I looked a proper so-and-so— but still . . . The photographers came in. Monty returned as the last flash bulb exploded.

He clutched at his collar, his eyes glazed with disbelief. "No, Grace! No! Not even you! *Grace*, you *wouldn't*, you *can't* have been fool enough to let them take pictures of you like *that!*" He walked round and round me wringing his hands. "Your hair, oh, my Lord, your hair."

"Ee, I don't know," I said. "I thought it looked completely daft myself. Still, you said I had to have a smart hair-do. So now, if you don't mind I'll dash into the bathroom and shove my head under the tap." Monty followed me dancing up and down in a frenzy of dismay. "You've only got ten minutes before the banquet!"

"All right, lad," I gasped. "I'm just washing all this muck out."

I rubbed my head with a towel, grabbed a hat and pulled it down over my wet hair and said to Monty, desperately, "It'll have to do." In five minutes we were at the Waldorf-Astoria facing the two hundred writers.

When we got to the huge reception room all talk stopped and everybody stared. I felt ugly and awkward. My mouth froze in a silly smile. I didn't know what to do or to say. I wanted to run away—and all the time I could feel a cold trickle from my wet hair dribbling down my neck.

Remembering it like that it was comforting to read the reports the next day. One of them said: "Having seen America's highest paid actress (Mae West) I felt obliged to see the world's, Gracie Fields. . . . She was late and she breezed in as naturally as a gust of wind. She flashed a big honest-to-goodness smile, acknowledged the introductions *en masse*, pushed her hat back with a broad comedy gesture and said something like: 'This makes me feel like a blooming queen.' . . . From then on there was pretty continuous merriment . . . she certainly looks like a hit!" I certainly felt like a damp, *very* damp, squib.

American journalists can be tough. They'd spread it around that no one would be able to understand my Lancashire accent, which doubtless accounted for one New York agent remarking gallantly: "De guy next to me says your accent's gonna be bad. I'm gonna tell dat guy waddya mean bad! It's okay, boy! She spiks English justa like I do!"

In Hollywood the first thing I wanted to do was to see the big stars' houses. Monty was very amused and drove me round. By the time we got back to our hotel, Hollywood was busy giving *me* the star treatment. My rooms were filled with flowers, from the very stars whose homes I'd been gawping at. The publicity men moved in. The big names started giving parties for me.

Next morning Monty bounced in excitedly. "You're going to see Darryl Zanuck today," he said, reverently. I was impressed. Even *I* had got to know about Darryl Zanuck by now.

We were to meet Mr. Zanuck for lunch in the studio's executive dining suite. "We must be absolutely punctual," said Monty. We were. We waited in the lounge leading to the dining-room. Every now and then a waiter would appear to ward off any innocent who happened to come in with the awesome words: "Excuse me, but Mr. Zanuck is expected." They always scuttled away rapidly.

Time passed and nobody came. Monty departed to see what was happening. More time passed. A little man with a tiny smudge of a moustache and a rather absent-minded air drifted in.

I was terrified that any moment the Great Important Darryl Zanuck would sweep in with his retinue and find this harmless little fellow cluttering up the place. I didn't want to see him trampled on, he looked a nice friendly little chap.

I cleared my throat. Nicer if I threw him out than that haughty waiter bloke. "Are you looking for somebody?" I asked kindly. He blinked at me. "Er—yes," he said. "Are you Gracie Fields?" "Yes," I said, "but just at the minute I'm waiting . . ."

The little man rubbed his hand across his face in rather a bewildered way. "Ah," he murmured. "I'm Darryl Zanuck. May I sit down?"

Oh, dear! But after a few minutes' talk I began to see the big business inside this little man. In a city shrieking with personalities, hair-tearing ideas, million dollar epics, Darryl Zanuck burned quietly like a small grey lighthouse firmly fixed on dangerous rocks. The waves might break around him, but *he* was never at sea.

"We'll have to find some stories for you," said Mr. Zanuck serenely. "I'll have some sent for you to look at."

It should have been as easy as that. Read some ideas, choose one, and work on it. But not in Hollywood.

"Zanuck says you're to have stories! Stories! Stories!" And at once my life became a whirligig of film-scripts, shooting scripts, ideas, treatments, conferences. Each new idea started in the morning as the best in the world, and was tossed away by midnight.

Yet, when I went to dinner at Mr. Zanuck's house, it all seemed probable again and no longer a mad-house.

There is an outstanding thing I remember about Hollywood hospitality.

It happened to me for the first time at Louis B. Mayer's lovely home. You go to dinner with thirty or forty other guests. Everybody is utterly charming, the conversation bright and slick, and the personalities shine.

Then you go into the big drawing-room where deep comfortable armchairs are arranged in front of a cinema screen. Everybody sits down. The lights go out. A couple of film shorts are shown, the equipment is superb, much better than the average town cinema. Then comes the main feature, usually a new film as yet not released to the public.

This is privilege, and comfort too. You lean back and enjoy the film . . . but gradually you begin to sense a strangeness in the room.

The film goes on, but in the darkness that surrounds you there are no whispers, no human rustlings, no red cigarette embers. Gradually you notice an empty chair, and beyond that another empty chair. Your host has gone silently to bed or on to another card game somewhere; his guests have slipped out as silently. There have been no goodnights from anyone to anyone. Hollywood has departed and there you are, with nobody but a servant fidgeting impatiently, waiting to lock up. And the film show rattles on unheeded.

I felt dreadful the first few times this happened to me, and until I learned that, no matter how much I wanted to stay and enjoy the picture, I, too, would have to slip out under the cover of darkness—and let the servants go to bed.

Hollywood doesn't give many parties for the enjoyment of a party as we know it. Folks are asked because they're important, they go because they want to stay important, to meet the "right" people, to please their powerful hosts. And the moment the cinema show starts the host can vanish without having to end the party too soon, and the guests can go without waiting for each other to commit the social error of being the first one to leave!

While Hollywood was giving me the treatment Monty decided that I should have some teeth pulled, in order to photograph better.

I had four out, then another four. Just as the studio dentist finished the publicity man came in. "Hey, Gracie! Charlie Chaplin wants you to have dinner with him to-night. Can you make it?"

"Yes," I said, "if it's soup!"

But the dentist took this as a personal challenge: "Miss Fields, I'll give you teeth," he said.

He plonked a brand-new set of false teeth into my mouth, straight on to the tender gums—and that night I dined with Charlie and his wife, then Paulette Goddard, and ate roast beef, Yorkshire pudding and roast potatoes cooked in my honour by a Japanese chef!

Don't tell me that Rochdale folk aren't tough! As I chewed I remembered the Old Folks' Treat in Rochdale. It is a dinner given for the real old 'uns, hardly anybody under eighty, with scarcely a tooth between them, but they always insisted on finishing up with cheese and raw celery!

I thought of them with every mouthful. It gave me courage.

I needed a different sort of courage on the night I went to have dinner with Eddie Cantor. He had invited me to appear on his radio show, one of the biggest in America, and Monty and Twentieth-Century Fox thought this would be excellent publicity for me.

"You come and have dinner with me and my wife, and my five daughters," said Eddie. "I think there's certain advice I ought to give you."

I went with Monty and Harry Parr-Davies. After dinner Mr. Cantor began to explain solemnly how much difference there was between English and American radio technique.

"You see, radio here is sort of—different!" he shaped a square with his hands. "Different, you see?"

Monty nodded brightly. So did Harry. Obviously they saw. I didn't.

Eddie Cantor went on. "Your entire technique—your approach"—he sketched a kind of Maltese Cross in the air with his hands, shaping it with the utmost care—"it must be different—like this—you see?"

Monty nodded eagerly. "Yes, of course, she must realise that." He gave me a bright look. I felt my mouth dropping slowly open like a village idiot. Eddie Cantor's hands were beginning to hypnotise me.

"So the thing is," Eddie continued earnestly, and by now his fingers were moving as if he was trying to dust the inside of a spiral drainpipe, "you'll need to re-model your presentation—so." He threw me a thoughtful frown, "Are you following me?"

"Oh—yes! yes!"

"Then would you like to sing me some little thing—just a brief song of some sort, to show you get the idea?" His eyes wandered to the piano and Harry Parr-Davies jumped up. "What'll you sing, Grace?"

I tore my gaze from Eddie's two huge, solemn eyes. They had me in a trance. He had managed to terrify me, though he didn't realise it.

What was I going to sing? Everybody was waiting politely. I couldn't remember the name of any song at all, except "Sally," which is the one song I would never choose to sing to show my vocal ability as it was always too simple and easy for me, being just a simple tuneful ballad.

"Sally," I said hoarsely. I saw Harry's surprise, but heaven help me, it was all I could think of.

Now when I am badly nervous I go right back to the kind of singing my mother taught me. I sing loudly, just like the lady off the halls who came into our kitchen when I was small and sang for us, and bust the gas mantle with the noise. My mumma thought it was wonderful!

In Eddie Cantor's elegant drawing-room I opened my mouth for "Sally," and sang so loudly that I nearly bust the light bulbs. Harry was thudding away at the accompaniment, his eyes and mouth screwed up in an agonised expression. I couldn't help it, shriek after shriek came out.

When Monty was very nervous he used to roll his eyes. I looked at him—his eyes were rolling. That finished me. At last I got to the end of "Sally" and said in a rush, "You're being very kind, Mr. Cantor, but I can't sing in your radio show, I just can't. I'm much too nervous, I'd make a mess of it. I can't sing in America—I want to go home!"

When we left Monty was in a despair of impatience. "This was so important to you, Grace! Whatever happened? Surely! Couldn't you see? He was trying to be so helpful."

"I suppose so," I said dully. "I know I made a fool of meself, but what did he mean with all that technique business?"

Monty hadn't expected that. "Well . . ." he began. Then he tried again. "Well . . . you see . . ." He frowned and tried for a third time, "Well . . . er . . ." Then we both began to laugh. We laughed till the tears ran down our faces. "I don't know!" said Monty between gulps of laughter.

Two Hollywood producers invited us to their ranch near Palm Springs for Christmas. It was like Capri without the sea. Snowcapped mountains on the skyline, and the hot desert scented by myriads of flowering cactus shrubs and date trees, stretching away for miles.

I enjoyed my first barbecue; broiled steaks and chops, beans and bacon, ranch-cooked muffins, salads, coffee, home-baked pies, all spread out across a desert garden, with a big moon shining above.

We were still at the ranch for New Year's Eve. There was another gay wonderful party with music and dancing and singing in the moonlight.

Monty had been dipping in the festive cup. He was very happy. "We ought to go and wish Joe Schenck a Happy New Year," he said. The assistant chief of Twentieth-Century Fox had a beautiful mansion not many miles away.

We left our gay homely little party and drove to Mr. Schenck's imposing home. It was alive with film stars and movie magnates. But "alive" is the wrong word. It was like a waxworks.

A Hawaiian band performed dutifully in one corner. It sounded dull and discouraged. No one was dancing. I tried to liven things up, and sang and danced. All the famous faces regarded me as though I was mad.

Buster Keaton heaved himself to his feet and we did an Apache dance together. We nearly killed ourselves with trying but all we got were a few sickly smiles. The Hawaiian band after this brief glimmer of life sank back into hope-lessness and fixed bright grins.

"What's the matter with these people?" I whispered to Monty.

"Shush!" he said. He was trying to conceal his little load of liquor and look very solemn like the others.

"Let's go back to the ranch," I suggested. "At least they know how to enjoy themselves there on New Year's Eve."

Monty drove me back. After a moment I saw him going off to his car again.

"Where's he going?" I asked. Somebody told me: "Back to Joe Schenck's place—there's going to be a high old time up there tonight, baby!"

"Are you daft?"

The man laughed: "It's a card game, biggest in Holly-wood."

Well, I knew that Monty was fond of a bit of gambling. We carried on with our own party and at last went to bed.

Next morning Mary Barratt came in to me quite worried. "Do you think Mr. Banks might have had an accident?" she asked. "He hasn't come home yet."

"I expect he's sleeping at the Schenck's house," I told Mary, and later I asked our host, "I suppose the game up there must have gone on fairly late?"

He laughed: "Going yet, I should say!"

Just before lunch time Monty's car came slowly up the drive. That was unlike him, he drove everywhere with a rush. I watched him get out. His body was all slumped, and his face very pale.

"I've lost more than I can afford," he said, and he spoke like a man in a dream.

"How much, lad?" I asked, thinking of something like a hundred pounds.

"Seven thousand pounds!" said Monty.

I got him a cup of coffee, stayed with him while he shaved. After a bit he began to feel better. Then his phone rang. It was Darryl Zanuck. "The game's still on, Monty— why not come back and have your revenge?"

All at once I began to understand why there had been such icy calm and lack of gaiety at the Schenck's party. Nobody had wanted to expend any energy, they'd been saving it all for the card game.

Monty look at me half inquiringly. "It's your money, lad," I said, "please yourself, I think you're *all* barmy." He went back.

He stayed away all the next day and night. After dinner on the third night I drove over to the Schenck's to see what was going on.

There was nobody about except the housekeeper, a tall sombre woman draped in black, looking for all the world like the housekeeper in *Rebecca*. She was walking round and round the swimming pool, and beyond it I could hear voices faintly.

I said: "Is the game still on?" She gave me a distant nod and indicated that I could go in.

It was a sight I shall never forget. At a huge table, in an atmosphere grey with tobacco smoke, sat the gamblers. Nearly all of them were famous men in Hollywood.

There was a white-coated masseur standing behind one man massaging the nape of his neck. Some had bottles of pep pills on the table beside their cards. There were coffee cups, sandwiches. There was Monty, pale and troubled, but obviously winning, at least, at that moment.

And in the middle of all this sat Constance Bennett, cards held gracefully in her left hand. Nobody massaged her neck. Her hair was perfectly tidy. Her gown seemed as uncreased as if it had just been put on. Her nose wasn't shiny. She sat like an alabaster statue, with two manicured fingers delicately touching her cheek, and her head slightly tilted in cool contemplation of her cards. With fortunes being won and lost all around her she looked like a lily on ice.

After a moment she must have felt my gaze. She lifted languid, startlingly clear eyes to mine, inquiringly.

"Have you been playing all this time?" I whispered incredulously. She nodded. It was such a little nod that the two fingers resting against her cheek did not disturb the cool marble outline of her profile. It was a polite nod. It made me feel as if I had come straight from a barn with straws in my hair.

I was fascinated. I just went on staring at her. I whispered to Monty: "Doesn't she ever go to the powder room . . . hasn't she moved at all in the last three days?"

Monty said nothing, but gave me a wicked smile, and went on playing.

I was told later it was one of the biggest marathon card games ever known in Hollywood.

Now it was early spring of 1938. "Time to go home to England again," I said to Monty cheerfully.

"But you haven't bought a house here yet," he objected.

"Buy a house here!" I said. "What me? In Hollywood? Have you gone off your rocker?"

"You should," said Monty. "You'll have to work out here again to complete your contract, you know how you dislike hotels, and besides, it's a good investment with dollars."

So I bought a small block of five flats in Hollywood. When I bought it I had no idea how grateful I would be for Monty's advice, or of the anguish which would bring me back to this property again during the war years. In any case I forgot about it for then, back in England, a letter, a very important-looking letter without a stamp arrived, which drove everything else from my mind.

Monty pounced on it. "Income Tax!" he said apprehensively.

I let him open it. "It's from the King of England," he shrieked.

"It must be a summons, perhaps I didn't pay the car licence; give it to me."

It wasn't exactly from the King—but it *was* a summons, though not the sort I was thinking of—it was one to go to Buckingham Palace . . . I was to be made a Commander of the British Empire.

Everything went wrong that morning. I had hardly slept I was so nervous. My hands were too shaky to hold even a cup of tea. My hair, as usual, went all awry and looked like a sackful of watch springs, and I had to get dressed up, something I've always hated ever since I was very small and fell in the brook in Rochdale when I was wearing my best, new, pale blue frock which dressmaker Polly Pickles had made for me. I didn't dare go home for ages and, when I did, I expected a good clout. Luckily for me it was the day Tommy was born and my mum didn't see me, or my ruined dress.

But that day put a jinx on me and ever since I've always dreaded getting dressed up, something always goes wrong. The day I had to go to the Palace was no exception.

Dad and Mother came up to London from Peacehaven. She sat, rocking placidly, while I struggled into my clothes. Dad kept calling the time through the door. "Forty minutes to go! Thirty minutes to go!"

I fastened the last button and whirled around.

"How do I look, Mumma?"

"You look all right," she said in her usual, matter-of-fact voice, "but happen you don't know your underskirt's showing—a good two inches of it!"

I *knew* something was bound to go wrong.

"Ee and I've got no time to stitch it up now," I wailed. "Quick, find us a couple of safety pins!"

My mother calmly helped me pin up my skirt, gave me a final look, and said, "That's all right, you'll do."

The taxi was waiting, it had been waiting ten minutes. Dad unleashed a flow of salty wisecracks to hide his own excitement. I could hardly breathe. But I honestly think if you had taken my mother's pulse at that moment it would not have been one beat faster. She had always said we were "going 'oop" and she took every bit of it, even a summons to Buckingham Palace, right in her stride.

I had to go into the Palace by myself. Before the war you couldn't take relatives in to watch you. I walked across the huge courtyard where a little crowd outside the railings recognised me and cheered. I was too frozen to look back. My smart high heels felt wobbly and I wondered if my petticoat would hold up with those two safety pins!

Big glass doors, wide red carpeted stairs, footmen in scarlet—I moved past them all in a trance.

"Please leave your coat and gloves," a woman attendant said, smiling.

Should I tip her? I was in an agony of doubt about it. What did one do in the King's Palace? "She's probably a duchess or something!" I told myself. "Best to leave it."

Gentlemen ushers were waiting for us. Beyond them was a great green carpet, big as a football field, covering the floor of the Royal Gallery, where the walls were lined with paintings.

We stood in a huddled group looking more as if we were to be hanged than decorated. We were directed to the Ballroom. It was enough to take your breath away, with a blaze of great crystal chandeliers, golden carvings, and ornamental ceilings glittering high above us. Near me was a burly police inspector waiting to get the Police medal for gallantry. He smiled wryly. "Nerve racking, isn't it, Miss Fields?"

An old lady who was going to be made a Dame said, "I hope the dear King isn't going to be so fussy as his grandmother."

"Fussy?" I asked. "Why?"

"Well, my dear, I think it was Queen Victoria who really began the custom of sending you back if you didn't do a proper curtsy."

Curtsy! I looked round wildly and saw Harriet Cohen, the pianist, among the crowd of us. "Harriet," I hissed, "is it a special curtsy we're supposed to do?"

"I don't think so," she hissed back. "But I've been practising for days!"

My knees went weak. I'd curtsied, from the stage at Royal Command Performances, but my legs had always been hidden by a long frock. But now, in a short dress—*and* with two safety pins in my petticoat! Supposing I caught my heel in my hem, and the whole lot came down.

I got one of those dreadful irrelevant memories that you do get when you're very nervous in moments of great solemnity. I suddenly saw my sister Betty when she bought a magnificent white bear-skin rug at a time when she was bent on having a real film-star's bedroom.

She used to sweep into the room in high-heeled mules and draped in a very filmy négligée, and regularly trip over the bear's head. It ruined her entrance and hurt her feet.

One day I went in and found her on her knees, very red in the face, pulling and tugging and swearing at the rug with all her might.

"Whatever are you doing, luv?" Betty had raised her flushed angry face, and waved a pair of pliers from the garage at me. "I'm taking this ruddy bear's teeth out," she

133

gasped. "So if he trips me up again at least the so-and-so won't bite me!"

I wondered wildly whether I hadn't better get my safety pins out, so that if I tripped up the so-and-so's wouldn't prick me into the bargain.

Then the National Anthem was played, and King George VI walked in. He was wearing the uniform of an Admiral of the Fleet.

The Lord Chamberlain read our names from a list in alphabetical order. A distinguished grey-haired man who'd smiled at me earlier went forward and knelt down. The King touched him on the shoulder with his sword. He was knighted. I suddenly felt a long way from ordinary life.

In a daze I watched Harriet Cohen go forward. She did two elaborate curtsies. The old lady who was to become a Dame did two less elaborate ones. Then it was my turn.

I blundered forward in a daze. I don't remember anything except a great wide smile on the King's face. He said something to me, and I would dearly love to know what it was, but I was too nervous to be able to listen properly.

I think I must have replied, for I do remember that he laughed and gave my hand a good-natured squeeze. He pinned the Order of a Commander of the British Empire with its Cross and rose-pink bow on to my frock.

As soon as I left the Ballroom one of the ushers came and took my decoration off and put it in a velvet-lined box. Not until I got outside, opened the box, and gazed at it, did I really realise I'd got my medal.

We had a family dinner party that night, with champagne and the lot. I remember the excitement, the family toasting me, and then someone asking: "What's the matter, Grace? You're very quiet."

I couldn't tell them; I couldn't begin to explain how I was remembering the actors' washing in the kitchen at

Rochdale; the day when we'd had to burn old boxes because we didn't have any coal and mother had insisted: "Tha'll not go back to t'mill, Grace, I will. You're going on t'stage."

I had my medal in my bag. I looked across at Mother, very proud in her new black evening dress, her hair beautifully done, a diamond ring we'd given her sparkling from her finger. As usual, and especially that night, she would have shut me up if I'd tried to explain, but what I wanted to do was to go up to her with that medal, and tell her, in front of the whole world: "There you are, luv. They should have pinned it on *you*." And so they should.

But I think my mumma really got *her* medal a few weeks later when they gave me the freedom of Rochdale.

We stood together on the balcony of the Town Hall with all Rochdale cheering us below, and if ever I felt proud I did that day, not of myself, but of my mother and dad, standing there and being honoured like a king and queen by the town where they'd married, worked, struggled and reared us kids.

I think it was the greatest thrill of their lives, and only Rochdale could have given it to them.

At this time I kept getting a funny feeling, as though I expected, indeed hoped, that someone, though I didn't know who, would suddenly say to me: "All right, Grace, that's enough, you can pack up now." I always felt so tired.

But there was no one to say I could pack up. The fêting and the work went on and on. They gave me another medal, the Order of St. John of Jerusalem, for the bits and pieces I'd done for hospital charities; they let me have the Albert Hall, which holds seven thousand, to sing in, in aid of a fund for the London hospital at Whitechapel, and then they made me a Life Governor of that hospital. There were shows at the Palladium again, another film in Hollywood, another one in London.

It was May 1939. I was talking to Rita Holmes, the wife of my dear friend Teddy Holmes who has helped me so much throughout my career. "I don't know what it is," I kept saying wearily, "but I'm so tired all the time. I'll just *have* to take a long holiday."

"I think you should see a doctor," said Rita. "Come and see mine."

Her doctor said I should go into hospital for a little check-up.

Before I came out of hospital I was to know that, for me, there could never be the love of my own children—for I should never be able to have any—and yet, for me, they would say prayers in the churches, and half a million people would write to me.

And before I came out of hospital I was to come close to the meaning of death and of heartbreak, and the meaning of love and of God.

I was forty-one then, and it was in that illness that I learned all those things which have carried me through my life ever since.

6

WHEN I was a kid in Rochdale one of my
favourite games was to hang on to the back of a tram as it
started off and run with it, till it ran me off my feet and I
had to let go.

As the tram gathered speed the excitement of keeping
up was wonderful, faster and faster and faster, your legs
went so fast you couldn't feel them. When the moment
came that you had to let go you were dizzy.

When I try to remember all that happened to me in the
last three years before the war I feel just the same way. Life
was the tramcar, and I hung on till it ran me off my feet.
Then I had to let go—and I nearly died.

Though twelve years of "top-billing" had earned me a
C.B.E., a fortune and a lot of fun, it hadn't helped me to
change much underneath. I was still as shy and awkward
about some things as I'd been in my Rochdale days. And
the thing that was bothering me most in the early summer
of 1939, just before I was ill, was a party I'd been asked to
give for charity.

Lady Allendale had asked if I would have the party in my
own garden and home; there would be four or five duchesses
there and maybe even the Queen would come to it, she

said. It had me proper bothered. They could have my home, they could have me singing for them, but if I had to be the hostess I knew I'd be nervous and do something wrong! I dreaded it.

When the doctors said I must have a minor operation I thought this was a wonderful way out. I can still remember my relief! "Now I won't have to worry about making a mess of giving tea to the Queen and all those duchesses," I said to my companion, Mary Barratt.

The surgeon, Mr. Searle, wanted me in a nursing home for ten days. "Seven," I told him. "I've got two Sunday Appeals broadcasts. I'll come in after the first, and go out in time for the second."

When the slight operation was over I felt more rested than in twelve years, perhaps even in twenty. My face seemed to have had the tiredness ironed out of it. Everyone said they hadn't seen me looking so well for a long time.

But, while I was looking forward to getting better and going home, Monty Banks and my sisters seemed to have been rounding up all the famous doctors in England, and Mr. Searle consulted all of them. Even the King's physician, Lord Dawson of Penn, was there.

I couldn't think what all the fuss was about. Then they told me; the little operation had only been preliminary; I had to have another, a very serious one. When it was over I should be unable to bear children.

At the back of all the work, the success and the laughter, I had always kept my own private dream that one day, even though I was now forty-one, there'd be a husband and children of my own for me, to make my home a real home.

I'd shared in my sisters' children, my orphanage children, and I loved them all, but I'd always longed for some of my own, belonging to me, that I'd know as well as I knew myself; my own kids who I could talk to, share things with, around whom I could build my plans for the future.

I'd had so much, yet I'd always been sure that sometime I'd have even more, those things that money can't buy, that only life can give you. The hours in which I had to tell myself: "Well, you can't have everything" weren't all that easy.

Then I remembered my second broadcast.

"You'll have to put that operation off for a bit, lads. I've got a date next Sunday."

Lord Dawson shook his head. "Utterly impossible, my dear young lady. I absolutely forbid it."

"Don't worry," said Monty. "Your brother Tommy's going to do it."

But I felt in a funny way that even if this illness was making me break faith with those things I had hoped to get out of life, it wasn't going to make me break faith with what life had given me. It seemed I'd been given—what shall I call it—this trust in me that made folks respond when I asked them.

That Sunday the appeal was for a hospital. That Sunday I, of all people, had reason to think of hospitals. When evening came I got up and phoned for a car.

"Better come with me," I said to Mary Barratt who'd done her best to stop me. "I may need a bodyguard to get out of this place."

My mother and dad were just coming in to see me.

"What do you think you're doing out of bed?" demanded Mother. "Get back."

"I can't. It's my broadcast."

"Our Tommy's doing it. Get back."

"I won't," I said.

There was a long silence. Then Dad said: "All right, I'll come with you, lass."

"Aye," said Mother. "Go with her."

penguin "spirit"

We reached Broadcasting House two minutes before the programme was due. Tommy was already at the mike, the script in his hand. Mary and Dad were holding me up.

"Are you sure you can do it, Miss Fields?" asked the anxious producers.

"What's all the fuss about?" I said. "Come on, I hate fuss."

Tommy was grinning, delighted. I did my appeal, and it brought in over twenty thousand pounds. That bucked me up a bit.

"Who would you like to do the major operation?" they asked.

"Him," I said, pointing to Mr. Searle who was a young New Zealander.

"Well, you know, he's not the highest in the land yet," they said gently. "There's Mr. . . . . . . , or Sir . . . . . . who are better known."

"He did the first, and I like the look of him. Let him do the next."

I didn't realise then just what a medical "First Night" I was shoving on to Mr. Searle.

Then I remembered another thing. My quiet Lancashire Auntie Margaret, who'd been with me for twelve years, was getting married—at fifty-one—and that week.

She had known her bridegroom for years, but never quite decided to say "Yes." He was an undertaker.

"Well, luv," I'd told her, "he's got a nice steady job! I'd say 'Yes'."

She had, and now I couldn't be at her wedding. Instead I was moved to the Chelsea Hospital for Women, and she and the family came to see me there, just when I was all dressed up in my long white stockings and operation gown.

Auntie Margaret, Dad and Mumma, my sisters Betty

and Edie; Mary, Tommy, Monty, Bert and Lillian Aza, they all stood there. I had to say something.

"Do I look smart in me Ascot clothes?" was all I could think of.

They all laughed far too much. Mother said, "Grace, you always were a damned fool!" and blew her nose very hard. Then they wheeled me away.

$$\star \quad \star \quad \star$$

"There's a special message from the Queen," they said. "'Please tell Gracie to get well soon.' Here's some red roses from Mr. Attlee, and more red roses from Lord Derby. . . ."

The little nurse was trying to rouse me. I didn't know I'd been unconscious for three days. I was floating in a grey haze. It was very comfortable. But the voice talking about queens and roses was trying to talk me back to life. It sounded very far away.

There was another voice, a commanding one. I thought I was back in the film studio. "Grace," it ordered, "open your eyes!" I couldn't. The voice kept on. It got louder. I opened my eyes and saw Monty. His funny round face crinkled into a smile.

monty at bedside

"Grace," he said again, gently, then bending over me, "the Bishop of Blackburn is here. He wants to know if you would like him to come in and say some prayers with you."

I tried to speak, I could only whisper, "I don't think I can," but they didn't seem to hear anything. I felt I was floating away.

I saw the Bishop of Blackburn, a tall gaunt man with kind eyes. I had met him on Blackpool sands, years before. He used to hold open-air services for the Bank Holiday crowds.

"Do you want to pray?"

141

Still I couldn't reply.

"She wants to pray," said Monty, and he placed my hands together for me.

The Bishop prayed; I tried to follow him, but I was too tired. Yet I wanted to pray so much. "I'm trying," I tried to say. The Bishop nodded: "It's all right; it's all right."

After a while he went away and the silence, and the relief, were beautiful. I said my own prayer: "Didn't mean to be rude . . . just didn't have the strength . . . please understand."

I think God always understands, and knows what you mean. Inside me, where the operation had been, I began to tingle. It seemed as though all my blood which had been lying still had suddenly started to course through me again. Then I went to sleep.

When I woke up I saw Mary Barratt sitting by my bed. Whenever the pain was bad, whenever I drifted away and came back again, I always saw Mary by my bedside. I think she could never have gone home. One of the most wonderful things I remember about that long illness was the sight of Mary there whenever I opened my eyes.

Next afternoon they brought me a newspaper, the *Daily Express*, folded at Strube's cartoon. It showed his famous "Little Man," with bowler hat and brave moustache, outside a hospital gazing up at a window, and holding a bunch of flowers.

There were two words printed beneath the picture: "Our Gracie."

Slowly I understood.

Then I did cry. They told me then that special prayers had been offered for me in churches of every denomination; newspapers had printed editorials wishing me strength to recover; nearly half a million letters were stacked in crates and boxes at the hospital and at Bert Aza's office. There were parcels, fruit, flowers and thousands more of everything arriving every day.

I felt I could never face anybody again. I felt so weak, so insignificant in my heart to be the centre of all this love. It seemed that nearly everybody in England loved me—and what could I do about it?

Half a million letters from people—yet I didn't know any of them.

They knew me—but *how* did they know me—as someone who could make them laugh, make them sing, cheer them up, perhaps help them a bit here and there. They didn't know me as the tired, inadequate woman I felt, and if they ever found out, I was sure they'd feel I'd let them down.

There was a radio in my bedroom and I switched it on. They were playing a favourite song of mine, "Come Back to Sorrento." I tried to sing it. Not a sound came out of my lips. Even my voice had gone. Now I couldn't even sing. I felt wrecked.

Then Monty came bustling in with a huge silver tray. He beamed at me cheerfully and waved away the little nurse who was wheeling in the meal trolley.

"Hospital food!" he said. "Damp potatoes, pale fish, ugh! From now on I—ME," he thumped his chest, "I shall be feeding this invalid. See!"

He whipped off the big silver cover from the tray. There was a bowl of steaming meat broth. He and Mary had been shopping for six pounds of prime beef. He'd borrowed a duck press from the Dorchester hotel, brought it to the hospital kitchen, and squeezed all the goodness out of the meat. This was Monty's invalid broth, the juice of a dozen beefsteaks! He fed it to me with a spoon.

From then on, every day until I left hospital, Monty brought my food straight from the Dorchester. Six weeks

in the hospital

later I was allowed to go home, thanks to Monty and the *maître d'hôtel* at the Dorchester.

But before I went I had something I wanted to give my surgeon, Mr. Searle. By now I realised what I'd done to him! I had no idea such a fuss was going to be made over my operation, how dangerous the operation was to be, nor what an ordeal it must have been for the brilliant, but as then, not so well-known young surgeon.

"I used to think *I* suffered on a First Night," I told him. "I can't imagine what the nerves must have been like for you, luv, before you got to work on me, so perhaps you'd like a present," and I gave him the original of the cartoon which Strube himself had sent to me. I prized it more than anything I had. It seemed right that Mr. Searle should have it.

Some time later someone sent me a replica of that cartoon most beautifully worked as an embroidery picture. I was so delighted to have it; no present has ever made me happier. I framed it, and it hangs on the wall of my bedroom in Capri now, yet I have never known who sent it.

The doctors told me I mustn't work for the next two years! "Go to Capri," they said, "and rest and rest."

We were going to leave Peacehaven anyway. Just as I was getting better the family told me something they'd been keeping from me. They were afraid my mumma was going blind.

We went frantic trying to find the best treatment for her. Mr. Rycroft, who had saved Monty's eye, and had taken care of Mumma through the years, thought it advisable for her to live in a good warm climate. The small block of flats that Monty had insisted I should buy in California seemed just the place, and how thankful I was that I had taken his advice. We arranged that Mumma and Dad should go there soon, and I went to Capri.

Monty and Mary came with me. "There's nothing but happiness ahead for you now," Monty kept saying. "You have nothing to do but rest and get better, and I shall be with you, and show you how to make olive trees grow in your Italian garden. I should like always to be with you, Grace."

I knew Monty very well by now, his humour, his cheerfulness, his courage. I thought there was nothing I would like more than to have Monty with me always. I knew that when he asked me, as I knew he would, I should marry him.

So we went to Capri and it had never looked more beautiful. Over the years we had all put a lot of love and labour into my little home and to me it seemed perfect. I loved every inch of it.

From my bedroom window in the morning I looked out on to a blue sea dimpling and sparkling in the morning sunshine, heard the gay songs and laughter of the two Italian girls who looked after us.

The air smelled fresh and clean, bright flowers splashed their colour everywhere and Monty, who was enchanted with the place, spent hours telling me where I should plant an avenue of olive trees and how I could use them as a wind-break for the plot I intended to have as a lemon and orange grove, and how, down on the rocky ledges beneath the house, I could build the most wonderful swimming pool and perhaps, a little restaurant.

I was eager to listen to all of this. Never in my life had I been so contented. Sitting on my terrace I was prepared to let the first real rest and idleness I had ever known flow over me. Now that I had nothing to do I began to realise just how tired I had been, and how much I had missed in the life of my own family by working so hard.

I remembered my young niece, named Grace after me, at Peacehaven one week-end, when she was resenting my work

145

as youngsters will resent anything which keeps an adult's attention from them.

Whenever I could I'd get down to Peacehaven on a Saturday night and sleep well into the Sunday morning. It was the only chance I got of resting from one week to another and my mother or Mary, would always bring my breakfast up to my bedroom.

Young Grace, who was Edie and Duggie Wakefield's daughter, would have been about sixteen then, and she'd never really heard me sing in a theatre.

My sister Edie had hated the theatre even though Mother had insisted that she went on the stage with the rest of us. She was in a show with Duggie Wakefield, and she'd come home, head over heels in love, saying she was going to marry him. "He's everything I said I'd never have," she told us. "He's not good-looking, he's got a turned-up nose, tons of relations, he's a comic, and he's on the stage, but I adore him." And she did.

Even so, marrying a comedian had not changed her attitude towards the theatre. She never went to one if she could avoid it and she rarely took her children.

Consequently I heard her daughter young Grace carrying on one Sunday morning. "Auntie Grace always come down here looking such a mess," she was saying, "and when she gets here she never wants to do anything except rest. Why should *she* have all this fuss made about her being tired, and she must rest, and she must have her breakfast in bed. My mother isn't like that."

It made me smile a bit. We'd sent young Grace to a posh school in Brighton, not far from our house, and what with that, and her mother disliking the theatre so much, and seeing me only at week-ends when I was always weary and wanting to sleep, I couldn't blame her for her little outburst.

My mother, surprisingly, said nothing but merely asked her if she'd like to go with her to a concert I was doing in London that Sunday night.

"No, thank you," said that young lady. "I don't care for singing much."

The following week I was giving a concert in Brighton. To young Grace's astonishment she found that many of the girls in her school were going. They seemed excited about it. Very quietly she asked if she could go too.

The concert was on a Saturday night, and it was a good one. I got a lot of applause and shouts of encores.

The next morning, Sunday, I heard my bedroom door open and sat up expecting to see Mary or my mother with my breakfast tray. There was the tray, beautifully laid, but it was young Grace who was carrying it. She put it down very carefully, then came and flung her arms round my neck.

"Oh, Auntie Grace," she said, as she hugged me, "I never knew you were like that, I never knew you could sing like that, I mean, oh. . . ." She bit her lip, then made herself go on, "I've been horrible," she said. "Please forgive me. I had no idea how hard you worked or what you could do. I'll bring your breakfast to you in bed *every* morning now, I'll do everything I can to help you rest."

I'd hugged my young niece back and thought, as I was doing so, how lovely it would have been if there was only enough time in the world to see as much of my family as I liked, and to do all the work too. What fun this sweet youngster and I could have had together, what happiness I should have got from being with Edie's daughter.

Well, now it seemed, there *would* be time, at last. I could have Edie and her children, and Betty, and all the people I loved out with me in Capri, as I'd always done. But now I could have all the time I wanted with them. It would be wonderful.

"You know," I said to Monty one evening, "this is the first time in my life I've really had a holiday here, I mean without songs to learn, scripts to read, concert programmes to plan, time-tables and all the rest of it, just a real holiday with Mary looking after everything, and me with nothing to do. It's going to be wonderful."

The next week war broke out.

The three of us sat silently, hearing Mr. Chamberlain's tired voice declare that we were at war with Germany.

All the lights in Naples Harbour went out that night, but I was thinking of the lights along Brighton sea front and Peacehaven, along the whole of my home coast. Britain would be in darkness too, and I wanted to be there, doing something.

I saw Monty was watching me. "I know what's going on in your mind," he said. "You want to go back and get into it, don't you?"

"I must," I said simply, and for once he didn't argue with me.

"Well, rest for as long as you can. I'll do all the packing for you," he promised and went away to get started on it.

Next day we discovered all movement of small craft in Naples harbour had been forbidden. The Italian fleet were at anchor, long grey ships thronged by busy little launches which churned between them continuously. We joined the crowd watching the activity through binoculars and telescopes from the heights of Capri town.

"I don't see any reason why we shouldn't *try* to make Naples in the speed-boat," said Monty. "Anyway, even if I'm Italian you and Mary are British, and you can break the rules."

Young Ettore Patrizi took us across. As we approached

the harbour we saw men in uniform watching us. I was worried in case we'd be arrested, but as we drew alongside, one of the guards threw a rope to us, helped us ashore, and saluted. Having seen our little boat come from the direction of the anchored battleships I think he had mistaken us for some Italian V.I.P.s, which was lucky for us. We rushed to the station and the first train that would take us across France to England.

For a few days we were busy arranging for evacuated mothers and children to fill up both the orphanage and my mother's home at Peacehaven, and then Basil Dean, who was organising E.N.S.A., asked if I would go to France to entertain the troops. I think I was the first one he asked.

"I know how much you want to do it, Grace," said Monty anxiously, "but you've only been out of hospital six weeks, and the doctors said you shouldn't work for at least two years."

"Work will be the best tonic I could have," I told him, and even though I felt pretty wobbly, I knew it was true. Maybe it wouldn't be so good for me physically, but for my mind and heart it would bring comfort to know that, in some small way, I could start repaying all the love and thoughts that had been poured out to me during my illness.

Monty, Mary and I decided to do the journey by car and before we crossed the Channel we spent the night in a hotel at Folkestone. As soon as we arrived a crowd gathered outside the hotel singing songs and bringing me flowers, and messages for the boys over there.

"You see what I mean?" I asked Monty. He nodded, but neither he nor I had any idea of the welcome waiting for me in France.

Now it was November and I was going to do two big concerts, one at Douai, and another at Arras. It was bitterly cold and as we drove along the French roads the car kept getting stuck in the mud and slush and we'd all have to get out while Monty and Mary pushed to get it going. I was feeling like death when the car got stuck again, and the next minute we were all mixed up with a long Army convoy. As we got out for the tenth time one of the lads spotted me and yelled: "Hey! it's Gracie Fields!"

That did it. Arras and Douai were to have been the first concerts for me since my illness but, instead, that first concert took place in the middle of a French road, surrounded by soldiers, tanks, bren-gun carriers and all the other paraphernalia of war.

fan encounter

The lads shouted for one song after another. Somehow, hanging on to the door of the car to prop myself up, I sang 'em.

At the two French towns it seemed to me they'd got half the Army packed into the small theatres there.

I am always strung up a bit before I go on a stage, but at those first two concerts of the war I was literally shaking with nerves, not least because I felt so weak that I wondered if my knees, let alone my voice, was going to stand-up to all that would be expected of me, and all that I wanted, so much, to do.

People often asked me what it felt like to be successful, and I used to tell them, honestly, that I didn't know. My work has never brought the relaxation of thinking. "Good, that's successful, now I needn't worry." Instead it has always been: "Phew! that went over all right, but that song, or that sketch, was so good, can I work up another to beat it?" for in show business there's no resting on your laurels, the next performance must always be one better than the last, and you can never forget it.

And if ever I felt that way I did that November night in France in 1939. But I needn't have worried. Those lads sang and cheered themselves hoarse and as far as I was concerned I was back in harness, doctor's orders or not. But Mary and Monty were on the doctor's side, not mine. "You'll be ill again," they warned, "really ill, and you haven't even given yourself a fair chance to get better yet."

I guess I can thank my Lancashire forebears for a good constitution, for, to tell the truth, I never did give myself a fair chance to get better through the whole of the war. There just wasn't any time. As for two years' rest, well, I did get two weeks, because Monty insisted that I went back to the sun in Capri again while travel in Europe was still possible.

I agreed to do this if I could sing my way across France *en route*, and that's how I spent Christmas, singing to the R.A.F. at Rheims.

During this time Monty and I had decided to get married, and we wanted to be married in England. But when we got to Capri there was a letter from my mother, from California.

She had already lost the sight of one eye and her handwriting was less firm, older somehow.

For the first time in her life Jenny, who had always brushed sentiment aside, now asked me to do something for her which once she might have dismissed as "soft." She said simply: "I want to see you wed, Grace."

Monty and I left Capri and flew to California, and my mother and father were with us when we married.

"Where shall we go for our honeymoon?" said Monty after the little ceremony. We'd been too busy to make any plans. We packed a few things in a suitcase and drove off towards the sea.

We stayed at a little wayside motel for the night. It was quiet, and clean, and nobody recognised us. Next day we drove on, but somehow both of us felt a bit isolated, almost lonely.

We had both been used to being with a lot of people, a lot of work, always, all our lives. In a crowd, among my big family, among theatre and movie folk, our companionship was complete, but alone together, it was not.

We were like two kids, always used to being with their family, and then suddenly left on our own.

Impulsively I said to Monty: "This is proper daft, wandering about like this, just looking at each other. Let's go back to our own little place and be with all the family. You're missing everybody as much as I am, the work, the noise, the lot."

That's what Monty and I had in our marriage, total companionship and understanding of the busy noisy world which was familiar to both of us. He squeezed my hand, gave a great happy grin and turned the car towards home.

As we got into the house the phone rang. It was Basil Dean, calling from London.

"I've got orders for E.N.S.A. programmes to promote goodwill between France and Britain," he said. "I want you and Maurice Chevalier together in a show, one in the Opera House in Paris, and one in Drury Lane in London."

It was the second day of our honeymoon. "We'll be home straight away," I said.

"Right, I'll fix it now," and then, as an afterthought, "are you fit enough yet to do all this, Grace?"

"I'll be there," I said.

I was still weak, and I had begun to realise *why* the doctors had ordered two years' rest, but I was prepared to do my best with that. I was remembering those half a million letters when I'd been ill. Here was the chance to answer them. I'd proved I could sing a bit, even if I couldn't dash around as I used to.

Chevalier was the gay unconquerable soul of France.

And Gracie Fields was chosen for England. It was something to be proud of.

Monty and I flew straight to France. We toured camps, the big ones, and most especially the small and isolated ones. "What we want for this job is one of those mobile Y.M.C.A. tea-vans," said Monty. We got it. Next day we were rumbling up the Maginot Line.

The troops surged round the little tea-car, the first they'd seen.

"Shove down the shutters, lads," I said, and began slopping out the tea. It was grand to see all those boys' faces when they recognised me: "Why, it's Our Gracie!" Little moments like that live in one's memory.

After the tea, the concert. This went on for weeks and months, all over France, until Dunkirk. That's when the ship they named the Gracie Fields after me, was sunk. That's when we had to go back to London.

Monty and I stayed at a hotel. It was there that the telephone call came from Lord Castlerosse, a great friend of Monty's, who was in Eire.

"Is Monty there? No? Well, give him this message will you—most important. Tell him he must come to Eire at once, or go to America . . . to do with his folks at home, d'you understand?"

I understood. It meant that Italy was going to enter the war against us, and Monty was Italian. Cheerful, brave, generous little Monty, my husband, would be an enemy of my own country.

When he came bustling in I had to tell him. He sat down and covered his face with his hands. "Oh, my God, Grace, this is horrible! What a mess for you."

"What a mess for both of us," I said. "I'm your wife. You're not going to be in this alone."

Ever since I had met Monty I had never known him to

let anyone down. I suddenly found it hard to speak. "We're in this together, Monty," I said. "We've signed on together, remember? But you must leave England quickly or they'll have to intern you."

"Not without you," said Monty. "If I leave you here, you'll kill yourself with work. If you stay, I'm staying."

"You can't stay."

"I won't go without you."

The arguments went on for ever.

This is no time to fight them out all over again. I loved my country and I loved my husband, and in the end I reached what seemed to me to be a fair compromise. I would do a nation-wide tour of war concerts in Canada to raise funds for the Navy League, if Monty would go to America, and then I would come back to Britain. At last he agreed.

As we reached Canada, Italy declared war.

When Monty and I met the Navy League officials at the dockside they were quite firm: "Mr. Banks will have to be interned."

"What about me?" I said.

"You, of course, Miss Fields, are English. Only your husband will be treated as an enemy alien."

"I'm his wife," I said.

"No one would intern you, Miss Fields."

"I'm his wife," I kept repeating. "If he's to be interned, you must intern me too."

They did not want me interned. I had arrived to do thirty-four free concerts for their fund, and was expected to raise several thousand dollars for the Navy League.

I stayed in Canada, and they let Monty go on to the United States where some time later he became an American citizen. He'd not lived in Italy since he was ten, and had taken out American naturalisation papers in 1922, but, like thousands of others, he had never bothered to complete them.

I did my concerts. They were such a success I was immediately scheduled for another lot. I was ill and exhausted, and I had to rest somewhere. I went to California for a week to see Monty and my mother and father.

no cancels?

At the end of that week the storm broke. Every British newspaper screamed that I had deserted my own country and taken all my money and one hundred thousand pounds worth of jewellery out of England with me. I was a traitor . . . I'd run away . . . I'd smuggled heaven knows what fortunes out of Britain.

I was stunned.

I looked at the small neat eternity ring with which Monty had married me, my watch, my bracelet, a small diamond clip which I wore on the stage, and a small brooch I'd been given when "my" ship, the *Gracie Fields* had been launched. I've never been one for much jewellery; that was all I had.

Of course I had taken some money out. I had to keep my parents and my two small nephews and my niece who were living with my mum and dad. There was my pianist, my dresser, my husband and myself—we all had to live; and though I was working all the time, it was for Britain. I was not earning a penny for myself. *—ENSA work*

As it was I had not taken out nearly enough money to keep us, and my brief returns to America during the war were only made to earn the minimum amount of dollars to keep my parents and their grandchildren in California.

Questions were asked in Parliament about me, and the Financial Secretary to the Treasury, Captain Crookshank, issued an official statement that I had *not* taken any unauthorised sum of money out of Britain. But this was not published till long after all the mud had been slung.

Monty read the papers in bewilderment. "What will you do about your concerts?"

"Go right ahead."

"But supposing they start howling you off, throwing things at you?"

"I'll have to go to find out, won't I?"

"You've got more courage than I have," said Monty.

I had tried to conceal from Monty how ill I still felt, or he would never have let me go.

When I returned to Canada I was besieged by reporters. "Why did you run away?" "Where have you hidden your jewellery?" "Do you consider yourself a traitor?" "Why isn't Monty Banks in prison?" "Are you afraid of the bombs?"

Every time I said the same thing: "If I have done anything I shouldn't have done, I will go right back and put it right. I'm going back anyway when I've finished this tour. But what have I done wrong?" But they never printed that.

I'd arrived at Victoria on the West Coast. They asked me to make a special twelve hours' flight across Canada to Toronto, in the East; twelve hours there and twelve hours back just for one show. I was feverish, dazed, unwell, and desperately unhappy.

When I got to Toronto the Mayor seemed certain he had an enemy on his hands. He was noticeably chilly.

There were two film stars making personal appearances for the same charity. The Mayor introduced them first. "I'm certainly very proud and happy to welcome you to Toronto," he said, grasping their hands warmly.

"And this is Miss Gracie Fields," said the Navy League official.

"How do you do," said the Mayor and sat down.

We were to go to a hospital first. There was apparently only room for the two film stars in the Mayor's car. I travelled in one at the rear. The film stars graciously inspected the wards with the Mayor; I was left to myself, so I sang, in every ward.

We got back to the Town Hall. The Mayor had some sort of speech to make. There was a huge noisy crowd. "There she is!" they shouted. My heart stood still—and then I heard them: "We're with you, Gracie! Don't worry, Gracie! We're with you! Good old Gracie!"

The Mayor couldn't get on with his speech. He kept holding up his hand for silence. It was the wrong thing to do, for the more he did it, the louder they cheered for me. "Sing 'There'll Always Be an England,' Gracie." The Mayor swallowed hard.

"Will you—Miss Fields—er please sing this—er—song—er—they seem to want you to sing?"

I've said before you must never let the emotion get at your self-control or your voice. But this was too much for me. My throat felt choked. I had to fight the tears. It took me a while, standing there while the cheers and the shouting went on, just standing there, swallowing, swallowing. I used everything I knew to get my voice back, to blink away the tears scalding my eyes.

"Come on, Gracie," they still yelled. "'There'll Always Be an England.'"

This, then, was the stuff their love was made of when half a million unknown people had sent it to me when I was dying. Here it was, real, understanding, pouring out to me, just when I needed it most.

If they would give it to me in Canada, then surely I must still have it in England.

This was the goodness of the everyday folk that I had known, believed in, and belonged to ever since I was a child. If they loved you they'd see you through thick and thin, like Monty had stood by me, like I would stand by

Monty. They *knew* I wasn't running away, and that was all that mattered.

"Come on, Grace. It's all right, we're with you. . . ."
Somehow I started to sing:

> *"There'll always be an England*
> *While there's a country lane . . ."*

My voice sounded small to me, a bit stumbling, my throat ached. Then, like a great warm helping hand, all those wonderful people joined in with me, carrying my voice along:

> *"Wherever there's a cottage small*
> *Beside a field of grain . . ."*

As we got to the last line I felt my voice free itself, in my throat and in my heart; it soared, leading the great multitude of voices to the last fine promise of the words:

> *"And England shall be free*
> *If England means as much to you as England*
> *means to me."*

The roars of applause and cheers went on for minutes, and for the only time in my life the only way I could acknowledge them was to stand there with my face turned away, trying to hide the tears I could no longer control.

When the evening papers came out they were full of photographs of the two film stars at the hospital. There was nothing of me. *press not on her side*

At the big concert that evening there were several performers. I was asked to keep my act down to fifteen minutes.

Harry Parr-Davies, my pianist, was smouldering with rage. "If it was me," he said icily, "I'd give 'em oompah oompah, stick it up your jumpah, and stalk straight off."

"But it's not you, lad, it's me, and we'll give 'em the best we've got in fifteen minutes." Then we were on.

All my life Archie Pitt, Bert Aza, Harry, Monty, had kept telling me: "You're a lousy showman, Grace, you never let the applause ride."

This is true. I always stop it with my errand boy's whistle. Any artist can encourage applause. If you let it go on too long you over-run your time and cut down that of the other acts following you. It isn't fair.

But this night, for the first time in my life, I let it ride. I sang with all the gratitude for the confidence and courage I'd been given that afternoon. I sang with everything I had in me to give. At the end of my fifteen minutes I just stood there and let the applause roll. Then I went to my dressing-room.

From there I could hear it thundering still. The management fetched me back. They couldn't get on with the show. People left their seats and crowded round the orchestra pit leaning over to shake my hands. They wouldn't stop yelling and cheering. They wouldn't go back to their seats. It went on for ten minutes, so Harry told me. He'd been timing it with grim satisfaction from the wings!

"All right," I yelled when I could finally make myself heard. "Listen! I'm coming back to the Massey Hall, for the Navy League. Come then, come again, I'll be singing then for two hours."

They came. When I returned to Toronto they held me as the solo artist at the huge Massey Hall for five nights, and it broke all records.

I wouldn't be boasting about this except that what happened in Toronto on that first visit hurt me, and, well, it was nice to be able to show 'em.

My first six concert towns were all up to eight hours' flying time apart. It meant being up at dawn, thundering

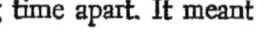

all day across the sky, and arriving in the next city just in time to be whisked by car to the concert hall, then a few hours' snatched sleep at an hotel—and the same thing all over again tomorrow.

I was so tired that the whole thing became a nightmarish blur of scenes . . . faces . . . concert halls . . . like shapes seen underwater.

Airports, officials, handshakes; ladies in furs, men in uniforms, speeches; Harry grumbling that there wasn't a good piano. Tiers of faces, applause, sandwiches . . . coffee that tasted of thermos flasks . . . tea that tasted of yesterday's thermos coffee . . . Harry grumbling it was a bad piano.

Scottish pipe bands shrilling at draughty plane halts . . . feeling dead . . . pulled in carriages through the streets by Navy boys . . . Harry grumbling it was the worst piano he'd ever played.

We went by night train to the little town of Port Arthur, and arrived at six A.M. Harry, pasty with lack of sleep, had dozed off. My head ached and throbbed. We talked longingly of the hotel beds awaiting us. Some men came on to the platform, officials from the Navy League.

"Would you lead the procession and the band through the town, Miss Fields, and wake up the people? It would be a wonderful boost for the concert."

"What, at six in the morning! I should think they'd cuss me."

"Oh NO! Miss Fields."

"All right then. Where? When?"

"Starting from the Town Hall in half an hour."

We couldn't wake Harry. The railway officials agreed he could sleep on in the coach which was shunted into a siding. A car would be sent back for him.

That brass band certainly wakened the town. It boomed and strutted through the streets. Windows shot up. Heads popped out. People stood at their front doors. It even wakened Harry. He left the train to find out what it was all about. When he did he was furious.

He tore after us in a taxi, his hair tousled, his collar crumpled. As he caught up with our official car he stuck his head through the taxi window. He was white with temper.

"You . . . you left me behind!" His Welsh voice was shrill, he sounded like an indignant seagull. "You! You think of nothing but your blasted audience!" It took all our tact and time until lunch to soothe him.   ⌐CBC ?

He was still in a rage when a radio interviewer came to talk to us. I told him Harry had been my accompanist for ten years. "No, I haven't," snapped Harry. The interviewer was amazed. "Is it a mistake then?"

"Yes!"

"Then how long have you been with Miss Fields?"

"Nine and a half years."

The interviewer laughed. "Oh, so you want to split fine hairs?"

"YES," said Harry, his voice recorded for all Canada to hear.

When he listened to the re-broadcast that evening he laughed till the tears ran down this face.

Those tours ended with the Navy League of Canada giving me their highest decoration, the Award of Service Medal.

I wrote then to Basil Dean to tell him I was now ready to come back to England as I'd promised, and do the same sort of tours for him.

In his reply he told me they were already snowed under with requests for my concerts, and he confirmed that my first Canadian tour had earned one hundred and seventy thousand pounds and the next one nearly three hundred thousand pounds.

On my way back to England the English Speaking Union asked me to do some concerts for the British War Relief in America. This time the newspapers said: "Britain wants fifty warships. If she will send us Gracie Fields we will give Britain all the ships she needs." *newspaper*

I had been away for thirteen months, and they said that in that time I'd earned a million and a half dollars for Britain. I'd worked against doctors' orders, and I'd worked harder than ever in my life. But, for me, the verdict was to come when I landed in my own country.

I got it, in Rochdale, and in London's Albert Hall; in camps, factories, and munition works all over Britain, where I sang, day after day for thirty-nine days. They cheered and shouted: "Good old Gracie." *— forgiven quickly Scandal ritual*

In Glasgow, where I'd sung to one shipyard, a rival shipyard threatened to strike if I didn't sing there too. They had no platform. I remember kneeling on top of the piano to sing. I remember the sound of their cheering. All the months of pain and hurt were wiped out in a few hours.

It was still only 1941. The war went on for another four years. In all that time, and longer, sometimes with Monty, doing sketches together, I sang for the troops . . . British, Australian, Canadian, New Zealand, American, all over the world.

All the time I wore khaki drill trousers and shirt, and an Australian hat.

When I try to remember the places we went to I feel like an atlas. Australia, New Guinea, Borneo, Cocos Islands, Christmas Island, Manila, Singapore, Rangoon, India, Okinawa, Bougainville, North Africa, Sicily, Italy, those are some.

I sang in jungle clearings and airfields; on ships and in dugouts; on football fields and railway stations.

When I start to remember the things that happened, well, "Gracie's War" would make a thousand stories, I'd like to tell just two.

We were at Bougainville.

I had a bad cold, and jungle ulcers; I'm always in the fashion, most of the boys had jungle ulcers so I had them too.

Though the damp heavy tropical heat was stifling, every flap and button of my khaki suit was done right up to keep any more of the variety of bugs and insects from biting me.

The General who had showed me the jungle clearing where I was to sing that evening, came up white-faced with a sort of dazed excitement.

"I want you to come with me *now*," he said. It was midday.

He took me to the huge clearing. Already it was packed with twenty-five thousand troops. With all the top brass I stood facing them. The boys must have wondered about the small odd-looking creature I looked, all muffled up in creased khaki.

The General stepped forward. "Men, at last I can tell you the only thing you want to know. The Japs have surrendered." In the second's silence of wonderment and before the cheering could start, he held up his hand. "I have England's Gracie Fields here. I am going to ask her to sing the Lord's Prayer."

He led me to a small wooden box. I got on to it. There was a movement as of a great sea—every man had taken off his cap.

The matted green of the tall dark jungle surrounded us, but above our clearing the noon sun seared down from the brilliant sky on to twenty-five thousand bare bowed heads.

I started to sing. "Our Father which art in Heaven . . ." Because of my cold I had to sing in a low key, but there was no sound except my voice. The hushed thousands of men in front of me seemed even to have stopped breathing. Each note and word of the prayer carried across the utter stillness of the rows of bent heads till it was lost in the jungle behind them.

It was the most privileged and cherished moment of my life.

where are these letters?

I treasure the letters from the many soldiers who have written to me since, telling me it was their most wonderful moment too.

We reached Balikpapan six weeks after the first Allied troops landed there. There seemed to be nothing for miles but burned jungle . . . oil tanks blown to bits. The Japs, who were still holding part of the island, had filled trenches with oil to burn the invaders as they landed.

Yet even here, as with most of the other islands, our boys had used bulldozers to clear a patch in the jungle for the show. They had made a huge amphitheatre bounded on one side by steep sandy hills, and on the other by jungle. Behind this the mountains seemed to be tipped with snow. "That's ashes from the invasion fires still settling," they told me.

Towards concert time the yellow hillside had all turned green. It was covered with thirty thousand troops in jungle-green combat suits, clinging to the steep sandy slopes. Then the swift darkness hid them. All I could see were their cigarettes glowing like fireflies in the rich black night.

"Strike a match, all of you, just for a moment," I called out.

Thirty thousand matches flickered, lighting up thirty thousand faces—then darkness again.

"Do it once more," I said, "and you in front, turn round and look back."

When they had seen for themselves the wonderful picture I was facing, I sang to them, and they sang with me.

*   *   *

It was good to get home, to England, to Capri. My little house there had been used as a rest centre for the American troops. Among the letters awaiting me was one from a soldier. "I took one of your books away with me, Gracie. I want to keep it. But, please, here's the money to buy yourself another."

I wondered if any of us could ever do enough for those lads.

I was in Capri on Armistice Day, 1945. There were to be two huge concerts in Naples, one a semi-religious, classical one at the magnificent San Carlo Opera House, and then a real slap-up free-for-all at E.N.S.A.'s Bellini Theatre. I was asked to sing at both, but at the former I was just to close the first half of the show singing "Land of Hope and Glory."

When the invitation came, I not only had the 'flu, but there had been no boats running between Capri and Naples for three days because of the huge seas. I waited to see if there would be any chance of getting across the storm-lashed Bay, but none of the boatmen in Capri would risk it, and not even the Americans, who were in charge of the area, would take the responsibility. Although I badly wanted to do my "bit," I was not a little relieved that, feeling so ill, I would not have to face the journey.

Then the Royal Navy telephoned. "If you're game, Miss Fields, we'll send a crash boat for you and try to get you here somehow."

"I'm game," I said weakly, "but I'm a rotten sailor. You'll have to put up with the consequences—but let's have a bash."

They had a bash. They wrapped me in oilskins and I spent the next hour wondering why I hadn't died a nice peaceful death in one of the jungles I'd been in lately—but we made it to Naples, with about fifteen minutes left for me to get to the theatre.

I was wet through, my hair was tousled and tangled, and to add to my 'flu, I now had the worst attack of burps I'd ever had in my life. "This'll do 'em good for Armistice Day, I *don't* think," I was muttering to myself as the car rushed me to the theatre. "Of all times and all days to be feeling such a guy as this."

"Do you think you can make it?" the manager asked nervously, as I burped my way to the back of the stage.

"Well, if I can't, it'll be the first time 'Land of Hope and Glory' has been sung with hiccups!"

But when I walked on to the stage of the Opera House to the opening strains of Elgar's glorious music, I felt as though someone had poured all the stillness in the world over me.

The house was crammed, not only with our own soldiers, knowing that the war, the fighting, the danger and the loneliness was now over, but with many Italians as well.

The immense sound of that mighty orchestra released something, I think, for all of us, something that perhaps every human being in those five years of fighting had held on to, no matter what his race or creed. This was the promise and the hope that one day the war would be over, and now, as we sang together, we knew that it was.

7

no mention of violet

NOW that the war was over, Monty and I couldn't stay in Capri very long. We had to start earning a living for ourselves again. Our bank balances were nearly at rock bottom.

We went back to California where my little American secretary, Neva Hecker, had been looking after my house in Santa Monica for me.

I had found Neva in America in much the same way as I had found Mary Barratt in England.

Neva, too, had first seen me on the films, but her first impression had not been exactly flattering.

She told me, when she wrote me a fan letter: ". . . I went into the theatre just in time to see a woman on the screen singing 'Walter! Walter!' and thought 'this is going to be dreadful,' so I went into the powder-room to wait till the horrible noise was over.

"When I came back you were playing a tender scene, and I felt sure it couldn't be the same woman. The difference in you intrigued me, so I sat the film through just to be sure that it *was* the same woman.

"Since then I've seen your picture sixty-six times."

It was a long intelligent letter and, as I read it, I sensed again the same warmth and integrity that I had felt when I'd read the first letter Mary Barratt had ever sent me.

As I had instinctively responded to Mary's letter, so I responded to Neva's, and answered it. She promptly replied and for quite a long time we wrote fairly frequently to each other. The more I read her letters the more I liked her.

Some time later, when I was appearing in her area, I asked her to come and have lunch with me.

Since she'd seen my picture sixty-six times I'd taken it for granted that she was a cinema usherette. But when the very shy, quiet little girl arrived she said timidly: "Oh, no, Miss Fields, I'm a secretary in a hotel."

"Well, you can come and be a secretary to me one day, if you want to," I said impulsively, and that's how I found Neva.

All the time Monty and I had been away she had looked after everything beautifully for us, and now she was wait- ing to help us pick up the threads of our work in peacetime again.

My own plans were straightforward. I would go on doing shows, concerts, and recordings. But five years on the stage with me, playing to soldier audiences, had re-lit the acting fever in Monty. "I'm just a big ham at heart," he said, "but my accent worries me."

However, there was a character part going in the film A Bell for Adano, which called for an Italian accent. He got the script and I made him practise. Everywhere we went I took that script. When he got tired and put it down, I followed him about the house reading it to him. I stood for hours in the kitchen reading it at him while the poor little man tried to cook. He used to put his hands over his ears whenever he saw me, or interrupt me with: "Let's go back to Capri, Grace, and finish building that restaurant,

GRACIE FIELDS (From a painting by James Gunn, R A.)

Behind the flowers and under the ticker-tape you can just see me! This was my South African welcome.
(Photo: Hausmann)

and anything South Africa could do, home could do too This was a welcome Newport (Mon) gave me when I went there to do "me knittin' " I seemed to give the police a lot of crowd work in those days

The Strube cartoon which I valued so much and which was published in a national newspaper during my illness

(*London Express News and Feature Service*)

"OUR GRACIE

(ABOVE LEFT) A curtsy for the Queen, now the Queen Mother Cicely Court-
neidge is on my left

(ABOVE RIGHT) A treasured picture from my Album, taken with the President,
Harry Truman, in America—and he autographed it for me

(BELOW) A scene from one of my early films, *Sing as We Go*

and here I am with Victor McLaglen in *We're Going to Be Rich*, which
Monty directed (BELOW)

Brother Tommy and I in my dressing-room at the London Palladium The big
smiles are because Tommy and I had such a lot of fun when we worked
together in variety   *(Photo Keystone)*

Mr and Mrs Alperovici—Boris and me One of our favourite photographs
                                                          (Photo Runis Ltd)

and the swimming pool . . . please . . . I don't want to make films after all!"

But he made it, and it was a success.

"You've done it, lad!" I said. "You'll be a star again before you know what's happened, and then we *can* retire to Capri."

"Yes, two of us, two middle-aged stars in an evening sky," he teased.

He put his big affectionate arm around my neck.

"I hope it keeps fine for us," he said, he sounded a bit wistful. Monty, always so full of bounce and energy, had seemed tired lately. I looked at him questioningly.

"Ah! you have to remember, Grace," he said, "when stars begin to fade there must be daylight coming in from somewhere."

I had to try to remember that for a long time without Monty. The next year he died.

When I lost Monty I was fifty-two. At that age you can remember the dreams you had at twenty, just as you dreamed them then. I could remember mine, but when Monty died I tried to throw them all away. They could never come true now, I thought.

That there would never be any children of my own, I'd accepted. But now there was no husband either, and now there would never be a home that could really seem a home to me.

For nearly two years I travelled, I worked, and then I worked more. The work went well; the folks laughed and clapped and it seemed I still made them happy. Perhaps life had married me to work . . . I didn't know . . . I tried not to feel or to care too much, nor to think of growing old alone.

But every time I stopped working and went back to

(handwritten: ⑳ monty as home)

Capri it seemed empty, empty of every dream I'd ever had for my home there. I couldn't bear it.

Desperately I filled the place with relations and friends, all the time.

I think most people would have found it hard to believe that I was lonelier than I had ever been in my life—for I was never alone.

My family were wonderful and came over to stay for weeks at a time to keep me company. Neva Hecker, though I did not need her as a full-time secretary any more, left America and got a job with the United Nations Food and Agriculture Organisation in Rome in order to be near me in Italy if ever I wanted her. My former companion, Mary Barratt, had worked with E.N.S.A. during the war and was now married to a talented scenic artist she had met then, called "Ding" Davey, and they came over to be with me too; so did my manager Bert Aza and his lovable vivacious wife Lillian. I had plenty of work, plenty of friends, always something going on.

I was no youngster now; all this should have been enough. It wasn't. I was totally lonely.

You feel a bit foolish in your middle fifties when you find yourself envying other couples, especially when you've had so much out of life, but I *did* envy them. Yet it seemed so silly that I was almost self-conscious in admitting it to myself.

But everyone seemed to be in two-somes. My sister Betty had her husband; her son, Tony Parry, had his wife and two children; though Edie's husband, Duggie Wakefield had died, she had her two children; my brother Tommy was married with his own young family, Mum and Dad had each other, and Mary had Ding.

They were all eager to include me in their happiness, but I wanted to be a "two-some" too.

It's wonderful to have a family and friends and to be able to have them all staying with you. But, no matter how gay and noisy the days are, at the end of each one there comes the time when there must be someone who really belongs to *you*, with whom you can talk about everything. It doesn't necessarily have to be a husband; it can be your child, or your best friend, but it seems to me that most people need that special relationship of "belonging" with another human being. Anyway I did—I had always needed it—yet somehow it had always eluded me.

I started trying to convince myself that as I hadn't found it now, the chances were I never should.

I'd been wise enough to know that what I wanted most out of life was a husband and a family. Well, now I hadn't got either of them, so I'd have to think of something else with which to fill my life—but I couldn't think of anything except more and more work.

Too often my mind would go back to the days when I'd been young and there had always seemed to be some solution to loneliness or unhappiness.

I remembered especially one Christmas nearly thirty years back when things hadn't been too happy between Archie Pitt and myself. The atmosphere wasn't going to make much of a Christmas for anyone, so, on the spur of the moment, I'd said to my mother, "There are six chorus girls going over to Paris for Christmas, two of them have worked there before. Let's go with 'em."

None of us knew anything about Paris, but that was just the sort of thing Jenny liked, and we went.

The girls had gone off to some sort of a *thé dansant* and cabaret in the afternoon and came back looking very glum.

"What's up?" I'd asked them.

"Well," they said, "the place was full of good-looking young men but none of them asked us to dance. And then we found out that the girls have to ask *them* to dance, and *pay* them for it, and we didn't have enough money."

"Pay a chap to dance with you? I never heard of such a thing!" I'd been outraged. "We'll see about this. Come on, we're all going out to a really posh place. I'll treat you."

We had dressed up in our best bibs and tuckers and gone off to some toff restaurant, eight women, and not a man in sight!

The waiters goggled, they'd never seen anything like it before. They put us all at one long table which seemed to make us even more conspicuous among the other people, *all* with partners, the men in dinner jackets and the women elegantly dressed and dripping with jewels.

But then, I hadn't minded the other couples at all. I'd had youth and self-assurance and when the six chorus girls had wilted a bit under the barrage of stares I'd told them: "Take no notice, we're here to enjoy ourselves and that's what we're going to do. Our money's as good as theirs. Come on, we'll dance with each other."

I'd started fooling around, acting the goat, doing a bit of mimicry and hitting a few high notes and Jenny, bless her heart, entered into the fun of it and did her bit too.

At the finish we'd had that restaurant in uproar. Men at the other tables asked me to dance with their *wives!* All the chorus girls got a dance, the proprietors gave us all the ashtrays and flowers in the place as souvenirs and begged us to come back again, and Jenny got kissed under the mistletoe and was as flattered as could be.

"Ah were the only one that got off!" she used to say when we recounted the story.

And how we'd laughed at it, and how we'd enjoyed it.

Then, that sort of thing had been a challenge, but now, past fifty, I was too tired and too lonely for it. Shyness has always plagued me, and I've always had to fight it—off the stage. Now I *minded* being on my own and without an escort in a crowd of people, and I think, if I had stopped to be honest with myself, I probably dreaded the pity of people who might say, "We'd better see that Grace isn't on her own, she might be lonely."

They couldn't realise that their company was no cure for my kind of loneliness.

In the summer of 1951 my head was so full of this problem that when Boris Alperovici came to my house for the first time I scarcely noticed him.

I'd filled my home with people, and I had Betty's boy, Tony Parry, and his young family living with me permanently.

With twenty-seven people all sleeping in the small bungalows dotted about the steep terraces of my garden (there's only one bedroom in the original house itself, where I sleep) and all coming in for meals, I never had time to get dressed until I'd organised my Italian maid and cook with shopping lists, menus, and general preparations for the day. This always took a bit of time because I can still only swear and sing in Italian—I can't speak it fluently. So, I was usually tearing around the place enveloped in a huge towelling bathrobe till lunch time.

When, in all this chaos, the kids bust the automatic record player it meant waiting weeks for someone to come over from Naples to repair it, till a friend said: "Why don't you ask Mr. Boris if he'll do it?"

I'd heard of this Mr. Boris from several people. Norman Douglas, author of "South Wind," the book which had first brought me to Capri, and who had become a friend of mine had mentioned Boris.

As Capri is an island, the frequency of its electricity is odd, and it is difficult to get pernickety things like televisions and radiograms successfully adapted to its current.

I'd envied the tone of Norman's electric gramophone. "Ah," he'd said, "I got Boris here, he did that. I was attached to the British Embassy in Moscow for a bit, you know, and learned to speak Russian. He's half Russian, so I invited him over to brush up my conversation, and while he was here I got him interested in this record player, and he fixed it up for me."

Axel Munthe, the Swedish doctor and most famous of all writers on Capri for his "Story of San Michele" had also mentioned Boris. He told me one day he'd heard me singing on the wireless from London. "I can never get London on my wireless," I said. "Oh, that fellow Boris came and fixed mine," said Axel. "He's some sort of an inventor to do with wireless, you know . . . he managed to get me London *and* Stockholm."

And so I'd persuaded Boris to fix my machine too. He'd looked a bit bewildered when he came into the merry bedlam that was going on. I just pointed to the machine and left him to it.

After that I went to London for a show, and the next time I saw him was at a party given by some Italian neighbours of mine. He smiled politely but didn't speak.

Then I went on a tour of Canada. When I got back to Capri I found the kids had broken the tape recorder which I use when I'm practising.

"Sorry," my nephew Tony apologised for his children, "but I expect I can persuade Boris to come and fix it again."

Tony did persuade Boris. When lunch time came I said: "What about a meal for that shy chap. He seems to like to eat alone and not with us. I suppose it's because he can't speak English."

"Good Lord, Auntie Grace, he speaks English," said Tony. "He was with the Eighth Army in the war."

I went into the living-room to apologise to Boris. "Here,"

I said, "I'm right sorry to have seemed so rude. Why don't you come outside on the terrace and eat with us? I didn't talk to you because I didn't think you spoke English."

The big-shouldered, dark-haired man stood up and towered over me, then gave me his gentle, shy smile. "Please," he said, "I am perfectly happy. You are most kind, but please do not trouble yourself about me."

"Oh, but I feel proper rude, I do really. Come on," and dragged him out to eat with us.

We all liked him, and as we sat chatting over coffee I thought, "What a nice chap, nice and quiet, and he looks kind."

We talked about Capri, about various people we both knew, about music.

The rest of my noisy party drifted off to swim and sunbathe; Boris and I sat chatting till nearly tea-time.

For the rest of that week while he was working at my home he always had his meals with us, and he and I always had a little chat after lunch.

I liked his quietness; his steady blue eyes, his unhurried, peaceful conversation.

On the Friday it was terribly hot. As usual the party had all gone off swimming. I'd been busy in the house. I suddenly saw Boris still patiently working with the microphone of the machine indoors; he looked very warm.

"Here," I said, "you've been working all the afternoon, come and have a swim."

"Ah yes!" he said—and then, "but I do not have a costume here."

"I'll get one of Tony's for you."

It was nearly dark, and the others were all coming in for a drink before the evening meal as Boris and I went down for our swim.

When we got back to the house and changed, Boris and

I bumped into each other in the corridor, and suddenly, he kissed me. I was so surprised and confused that when he let me go and whispered: "I'll see you tomorrow," I could only nod.

I joined my gay noisy houseparty thinking: "Oi! Oi! another of those sophisticated ones, eh . . . didn't think it of him somehow . . . now I'll have to put on an act and try to pretend to be sophisticated too, I suppose, and brush the whole thing off."

For some reason I felt disappointed. I realised I'd got used to spending the afternoons talking with Boris; I liked him enormously. I had never expected that he would suddenly do something like that. I felt let-down . . . or did I?

After all, it hadn't been a cheap kiss . . . had it? No, he had never seemed to be that sort of person. Had he really *wanted* to kiss me? If I knew that he had really wanted to, then would I be glad that he had?

I got in such a muddle that the next day I took Tony's small son to Naples with me to try and put the whole thing out of my mind. After that I was going to England—so that would be the end of that.

But Boris turned up to say good-bye to me—and suddenly I was embarrassed at seeing him. I didn't know what to say. He seemed that way himself, shy, embarrassed.

That's what did it, his shyness. Underneath all the froth and bubble I'm shy too; I liked the shyness in him, and particularly then. Suddenly I knew: if it had been a cheap kiss, a casual sophisticated embrace, he wouldn't have come back, despite his awkwardness, to say good-bye to me. I saw I didn't have to put on an act of being bright and brittle. So we didn't talk very much, and when the moment came for him to leave he bent over me and gently kissed me on my cheek.

There was so much respect in the way he did this that,

176

for that instant, I felt like a queen. Then I went to London to play four weeks at the Palladium.

Well, I've had many crazy weeks in my life, but none quite so crazy as those. Everything seemed absurdly wonderful . . . the London buses, the faces of people in the street, the thought of the journey back to Capri, the songs I sang. And all the time I kept thinking of Boris.

"Stop it, you daft fool," I kept telling myself . . . but I didn't listen to myself.

Somehow I just had to talk about him to people, though I tried to pretend it was all a big joke.

"What would you say if I married a Russian?" I asked Bert and Lillian Aza. They laughed. "What! And cause *another* international situation?" teased Bert.

I tried it out on Mary and Ding. "You know, I think I'm proper struck on this chap," but Mary just laughed too. "It's because you're back to being your old self, Grace, you're bubbling over again, just like you used to, it's wonderful."

It was, but I doubted if it was just because I was feeling better . . . I hadn't been feeling ill!

I telephoned a Russian woman I knew, Mrs. Esther Rifkin, who used to make a lot of blouses for me: "I'm not wanting a blouse this time, Mrs. Rifkin, but could you tell me how to say 'I love you' in Russian, 'cos I've got a feeling I may want to say it!"

The astonished Mrs. Rifkin taught me the words: "Ia tebia liubliu."

When I got back to Capri there was no sign of Boris, and my nephew told me he hadn't been near the place for two months. Then I bumped into him in the Piazza, our little town square. He was carrying some beautiful Italian tiles. When I admired them he asked me if I would like to see them made; his friend, a lawyer, made them for a hobby, and his pottery was only at the foot of the hill.

I went with him. At the end of that afternoon when we parted I went half-skipping, half-running down the steep hill to my home. I was singing . . . yes . . . the sort of words any starry-eyed young girl of seventeen would be singing . . . "I'm in love, I'm in love, I'm in love with a wonderful guy!"

great visuals

I had no special reason for feeling this way. Boris hadn't said he loved me: I couldn't even be sure I loved Boris; all I knew was that it had been wonderful to see him again, and that he couldn't have looked more pleased to see me. And going up the hill he'd put his arm round my waist.

I hoarded every gesture and sentence of that afternoon . . . and for the first time in years I looked forward to that moment when I could be by myself to think them all over.

I was very severe when I thought them over. This couldn't be love, it was probably just an antidote for loneliness; this couldn't be love, I was too old to fall in love; this couldn't be love, if Boris had wanted to fall in love he surely would have done so long before now. How long would it be before I'd see him again!

He met me walking up to the town, I was going to buy some tangerines for the children. "Come and pick them in the garden of a friend of mine," said Boris. I went home without any tangerines . . . I forgot them, because that's when Boris kissed me again, and he'd asked me to tea the next day.

But it rained, and it went on raining for four days, and I was too shy to go in the rain, "It'd look as though I was running after him," I thought.

Instead Tony and I went walking and suddenly Tony said: "Let's go and see what old Boris is doing," and vaulted over a low wall we were passing. In a moment Boris came to the gateway, smiling, and invited us in. There was a woman in his bungalow hanging clean curtains; she was nice looking. I was certain she was his lady-friend, and the once shining wet day became dull and dreary.

When, a few days later, I found out that the good-looking woman was married, and that she and her husband had been friends of Boris's for nearly thirty years, the relief and the happiness were so wonderful that I made up my mind. I would ask Boris if he wanted to marry me, for I knew by now that he would never overcome his shyness enough to ask *me* to marry *him!*

And I knew by now too, that I was in love, for the first time in my life.

I had loved Monty, and he had loved me, and we had had a life together of warm companionship and understanding which, if he had lived, would have bound us together contentedly.

Monty and I had met through our work; we liked each other both as actress and director, and as people. We came from the same poor beginnings; we had the same sense of humour; we had both been knocked about a bit by life, we shared the same professional worlds. He gave me the leadership and managing which I needed; I gave him the laughter and friendship he liked.

We married because we enjoyed being together; it was a good marriage and we loved each other. It does not detract from that marriage one whit if I say that we were never "in love," which is something additional to love.

Our marriage was never a mad passionate affair of the heart which swept either of us off our feet, it was more the continuation of a rich affectionate partnership into the closer bonds of marriage.

When this ended with his death I was bereft not only of my husband, but of my best friend in the world, for that

179

is how I had always thought of Monty. And I was a lonely woman with an empty future at an age when a woman needs to know that her future shall neither be empty nor without love.

And now, just when I thought everything was over for me, I knew I was in love properly, and wholeheartedly.

All the love stories I'd ever read, all the sentimental songs I'd ever sung, I really understood now, for the first time in my life. I was astonished. When I was seventeen I'd often wondered whether my heart would ever bump at the touch of someone's hand; whether I'd ever shut my eyes and see only one person's face. *understands the songs now –*

Now those things were happening to me for the first time, and they were none the less precious for happening so late. I wasn't going to waste any more time by not having the courage to take them when, perhaps, they could be mine for the asking.

A few weeks later I asked—and Boris said yes.

We agreed to marry each other when all I really knew about him was that he was half Russian, that he was some sort of an inventor, that he'd lived in Capri for thirty-three years, and that he had never been married before.

Apart from my public life he knew very little more about me.

Since neither of us were children we both knew the risks we were taking; it could have been an Indian Summer romance for both of us—and over as quickly; we could have found that, despite our feelings for each other, it would be impossible to reconcile our two worlds, mine so full of people and travel, and his so full of solitude and books.

And Boris was not unaware of the criticisms and comments which such a marriage would bring. I knew this when I decided I must ask *him* to marry me . . . the first thing that some people would say of any man who married me would be: "Oh, he's married her for her money!" I knew that was why he would never propose to me.

Yet, in spite of all this, we both seemed to know instinctively that it would work out.

So we got married first, and started finding out about each other's lives afterwards . . . in fact we didn't have much time to do so before.

I mentioned marriage to Boris a few days before Christmas.

We'd been shopping in the Piazza. He was walking down the dark steep hill with me to my home. The darkness, and the fact that he couldn't clearly see my face, gave me courage.

"Have you ever been married, Boris?" I said, as casually as I could.

"No, Grace."

"But perhaps there's someone you love?"

"Yes," he said slowly. "Yes—very much."

My heart gave a lurch. "Who is it?"

"She's a very nice person—very nice."

"Are you in love with her?"

"Yes, I told you, very much."

I had to risk it. "Well, tell me who she is," I asked, and Boris stopped walking, and looking straight ahead of him said in a low voice, "You know very well that it's you."

"You really *mean* me?"

"Yes."

"Then does that mean that you would marry me?"

He started to walk on slowly again, without speaking. Then he said, "Yes, it means that I would—but I think it would be a mistake. You are a big star; they call you 'Our Gracie'; you belong to so many people, but I would like my wife to be *my* Gracie, and I do not think that would be possible."

I wanted to pour out a torrent of words, to try to explain that being "Our Gracie" wasn't the same as being one particular person's Gracie, and it was just this that I had wanted all my life. But I was too shy, too frightened, and too moved, to say a word.

Boris stopped walking again and adjusted the great bundle of Christmas parcels he was carrying for me.

"You're famous and known to all the world," he said quietly, "I'm simply a grey person belonging to nobody, with no family now, and no country.

"The country I was born in, Bessarabia, doesn't exist any more. It was on the frontiers of two different worlds, Latin and Slav, everything is a mixture there. . . ."

"Yes," I interrupted, "and you're a mixture too, a nice one."

"Perhaps not so nice," said Boris ruefully. "You see, with you I will be afraid to become a husband. I would be the husband of Gracie Fields, and I will resent this. I would want Gracie to be the wife of Boris, just Boris's wife."

In his careful English he was putting into words everything I'd always longed for, but still I couldn't explain. I could only say, "Yes, but we love each other, don't we?"

"I believe this to be so," said Boris, so seriously that even his quaint phraseology could not make me smile. "But my world is small. In one month, in twelve months, I will still be in Capri, just the same as I have always been. But you—you will be in the crowds. Perhaps this is just a Capri romance; we have both seen many of them, they last as long as the little holiday in your heart, they are a lovely souvenir. I hope this may be a pleasant souvenir for you."

"Boris . . ." I said, "I don't mean . . . I'm not . . ." Oh, dear, did he think I was just a rich, spoiled, middle-aged film star, playing out a romantic whim even to the finale of a proposal. But he interrupted me.

182

"Look, Grace," he said, gently, "it will be a joy for me to know that you would still remember this . . ." and I believed him, and I was more sure than ever that I wanted him to marry me . . . "but in a year, marrying Boris will seem to you a crazy idea." He went on, "Perhaps it is that great artists are not born for a married life, they have to give so much to others they cannot give just to one."

We had reached the gates of my home. In the short walk down from the Piazza, Boris had spoken all those things I had always found it impossible to put into words; he wanted from me all those things I had always wanted someone to want from me—and now I couldn't tell him so.

I wanted to tell him that, just because you're famous and need to "give out" to other people all the time, you especially need someone of your own to love and be loved by. But I couldn't say it. I was still unsure. Perhaps, after all, he was trying to refuse me. I was too afraid to say any more. I just said good night and went in.

Though we saw each other every day that week, neither of us mentioned marriage again, yet we had only to look at each other to know we were in love.

On Christmas Eve I had a huge party, all the people who were staying with me, and just about all my friends in Capri too.

The island has a Christmas Eve ceremony which I have always loved; the shepherds from the Abruzzi hills come across from the mainland, dressed traditionally in their wide, black capes. They bring their bagpipes, enter your home, and play and sing prayers to the Madonna.

Their entrance brought a lull in the noisy cheerful party, and my guests stopped to listen.

I was looking for a shawl to put round my shoulders, and Boris wrapped it round me. "After Christmas you're going

away again, aren't you?" he said, and he looked so sad, as
sad as I felt at the thought of leaving him.

I suddenly put my head on his shoulder, I think for some
sort of comfort, and thought a bit wildly: "I'll ask him
again—now—and if he says again it would be a mistake, I'll
know it's all been a foolish fancy."

I moved away from him: "Did you mean *all* you said the
other night . . . when I asked you . . . well . . . you
know? . . ."

"Yes," said Boris.

"And the bit about it being a mistake, did you mean that,
too?"

"No!" said Boris, "no, I didn't mean it, not if you feel
about me as I do about you. You're going away again, and
I feel lonely even before you've gone."

I took a deep breath. "You're sure?" I said as steadily as
I could. "Because if you're sure, I'm going to announce our
engagement now!"

"You are joking," said Boris, his face hurt and bewildered.

"I'm not, lad! I was never more serious in my life!"

It took only one second to see that hurt baffled look leave
his face and a smile begin before I put my arm round his
shoulders and gave the loudest errand boy whistle of my
life to hush the chatter.

"Everybody!" I yelled. "Listen! Boris and I are engaged!"

And what did my handsome Boris do? Did he pick me
up in his arms? Did he make a fine speech? No! It was the
first time he'd heard that whistle. When I turned round to
present him to the world he couldn't speak for giggling, he
was giggling like a schoolboy!

The champagne corks started to fly. Somebody must
have sneaked out to my telephone and phoned the local
reporter. In less than ten minutes it seemed to me there was

a photographer in the room, and the phone started ringing all the time.

"Here," I gasped to Boris, "come and talk Italian to that operator and tell her to get me a line to London before any more calls come in. I must phone Bert and Lillian Aza and my family and tell 'em. They'll be furious if they read it in the newspapers first."

The uproar went on. Somewhere around two A.M. on Christmas morning a dismayed Boris said that the little post office up in the square had had to send out and wake up their daytime staff because of the sudden traffic on the lines. By Christmas Day proper all the staff had a full working day because of all the telephoning and telegrams. Boris went up there to apologise to them.

About three A.M. I went back to Boris. "Here," I said again, "they want to know what me married name's going to be. I can't be called Mrs. Boris, what's your other name, luv?" He had to spell it to me—ALPEROVICI.

The chaos went on non-stop until we got married a few weeks later. Capri was so full of newspaper people that Boris and I fled to Rome to escape them. But there was no escape.

My main memory of those days is Boris saying in a crosser and crosser voice: "I am *not* marrying a famous star: I am *not* marrying a rich woman; simply I am marrying the woman I love."

He had never been used to crowds, people, pressmen; I was terrified that all the hub-bub would make him decide it *was* a mistake after all. Instead, I found out that he knew some pretty nifty English swear words.

"Boris!" I said in admiring astonishment when we'd really had a basinful of press questioning one day: "You really *can* speak English, where did you learn that?"

"Grace," answered my surprising husband-to-be, "I can

185

speak eight languages, but I swear best of all in English. Your Army sergeants taught it all to me. But never before have I dared to use it in front of a lady!"

"Well dare away, luv," I said. "After being in the theatre all me life, it sounds just like home from home!"

We did all we could to escape a noisy wedding. I had always wanted to be married in a church, and especially in the little church in Capri, and I didn't want the ceremony to be spoiled by a lot of quarrelling and questioning between hundreds of press boys.

I was willing to see them afterwards, I was grateful that they still wanted to take notice of me, but I *did* want just my marriage ceremony to be quiet enough for me to really listen to the words of the service—to feel their meaning as they were spoken.

To this end we got married two days later than we had planned and we made a secret dash over from the mainland back to Capri by boat, and thence straight to the church, very early in the morning.

The whole thing was such a rush and muddle that the press boys *did* succeed in following us, and my nephew's wife, Peggie, and my dear friend, Mary, missed the wedding altogether and only got to the church from my house just as we were coming out, whereupon they both burst into tears.

I'll admit that I *had* thought of the moment when Boris and I would drive away from the church, as man and wife; I *had* pictured that we would hold hands, that then I would know I was married, and that he would say something romantic and tender to me that I should remember for always.

Well, you can't get too soft at any age, for it never works out. There was Boris and me squeezed in the back of our wedding car with Mary and Peggie jammed between us, both of them crying their eyes out, and both of us trying to console them.

"We only did it to avoid the press boys," we tried to explain. "We thought we'd get the message to the house in time for you to get to the church. . . ." We had to shout, there were so many press boys and people following us.

But Peggie, and especially Mary, were both inconsolable. "I never thought I'd miss seeing you married, Grace," sobbed Mary.

She was so upset, as was everyone else at my house when we got back there that, in the end, all strung up as I was, I joined in and had a good cry too! We had a real wake, with everybody trying to comfort everybody else. "Oh, yes," I sniffed, the tears pouring down my face, "I'm terribly happy!" We quite forgot poor Boris!

At ten o'clock that night he came up to me with such a forlorn face. "Grace," he said pathetically, "if all the crying is over now, do you please think I could have something to eat? I've only had one cup of coffee all day!"

I awoke very early the next morning and my husband was gone! He was nowhere in the house.

In a panic I threw on a dressing-gown . . . I don't know what I thought . . . I think I had visions of a man bowed down by the realisation of the terrible mistake he'd made in sacrificing his tranquil life of solitude for marriage to a woman pursued by publicity and surrounded by a bevy of weeping females on her wedding day.

I half-expected to find him pacing the terraces in an effort to shake off his gloom.

I went out into the gardens looking anxiously for him. I searched everywhere. Half an hour later I saw an incredibly filthy Boris climbing up the steps from the empty swimming pool which is far below my own private gardens, nearly at sea-level. He waved and called up to me, his face alight with smiles.

I ran to him. "Boris! Where have you been?"

Boris looked down at me, looked at his dirty hands, hesitated, then put his arms round me and gave me a great hug.

Then he said, "I have been to do something that is my way of saying thank you, to everybody, and everything, Grace."

I looked at him in bewilderment. "I have been to put the underwater light in the pool," he said—and then I didn't know what to say.

In only seven weeks' courtship Boris and I had little time in which to find out very much about each other before we got wed, but he had asked me briefly about my marriage to Monty, and I had answered him honestly. Boris had met Monty and the last time had been when Monty had particularly wanted some ingenious form of underwater lighting planned for the swimming pool.

Boris had designed a scheme which Monty wanted to adopt, but first Monty had to go off to America; then the constant rows that went on over the construction of the pool had held up the building; then Monty had died.

The completion of his beautiful swimming pool had been one of Monty's dreams, and he had never lived to see it. Boris knew this. On the first day of his marriage to me he had got up at dawn, put on his overalls, and in the still beauty of a Capri spring morning had gone down to the silent pool and worked for three hours, putting in the complicated lighting system Monty had always wanted.

"I wanted somehow . . ." said Boris, almost inarticulate for once, "somehow I wanted to say thank you to him for giving you happiness . . . for the happiness I have found

. . . for . . ." he floundered for the words. "You think I am very ridiculous?" he ended shyly.

I looked up at the man I'd just taken for better or for worse. "No, lad," I said, "I don't think you're very ridiculous, I just know how right I was to ask you to marry me." And we went in to have breakfast.

8

WE HAD our honeymoon by courtesy of my two Alsatian dogs who had a full-time job barking their loudest to keep away the dozens of people who tried to get in and see us the first few days after we were married.

But Boris and I did manage to get some time to ourselves and, gradually, we began to find out all those things about each other's lives that most people find out *before* they are married.

Not long after our wedding I re-read, many times, a letter I had received from Edwin Cerio, my distinguished neighbour in Capri.

It is a little difficult to try to explain the exact position the Cerio family hold in the esteem of the island, not only as an old and aristocratic Italian family, but also because of their fine record of services to their country in the arts and sciences.

I suppose you might have called Edwin Cerio the "uncrowned king" of Capri. When Princess Margaret came to visit our island, there was no question but that it should be he who would have the honour of entertaining her.

Few people in Capri know the family intimately. They keep very much to themselves, and I had only met Edwin a few times before I announced my engagement to Boris, though I did know by then that Boris had spent nearly all his adult life with the family, and was practically regarded as a sort of adopted son by them.

So I was very touched when I received a letter from Edwin.

where is the letter?

"Dear Gracie,

Of course I am much flattered by the Christmas greetings sent by my future 'daughter-in-law' as you have playfully styled yourself, but which I feel very deeply, as it concerns one of the few men for whom I have a very great affection.

"You may know what Boris, for the last twenty years or more, has been for my family, which has become his family; how helpful he always was, and how we all appreciated his brilliant brains, but, more than anything, how we valued his stout heart and relied on his unswerving, true, lovable character. He is a ROCK.

"Personally, I know of no other man in whom intelligence, resourcefulness, profound technical knowledge and constitutional honesty are so perfectly blended with disinterestedness and reliability.

"Being so fond of him, though I never was very demonstrative about it, it makes me happy to know he has such a worthy and splendid purpose to which to devote himself now.

"By giving him the opportunity of meeting you life has handsomely rewarded him for all the sterling qualities of his character, his many struggles, and his hard work.

"My admiration for your genius and your art, dear Gracie, are shared, I know, by great crowds of people. But I would be very happy and proud, if, in addition to that admiration,

I may be allowed to express my affectionate devotion for the lovable generous woman who is going to be Boris's wife."

Probably few women have ever had such a letter about the man they are going to marry, and I was very proud of it.

But I had often wondered how it was that Boris should have gone to live with the Cerios and to work for them. "Tell me," I said to him one afternoon. "You know now how and why I first came to Capri. Tell me how you did."

So Boris told me. His father had been an architect in Bessarabia in the early 1900s which was then a country of mixed population, half Roumanian, half Russian.

His mother had died when he was three, his father when he was seven, so Boris was brought up by his two elder sisters until he was seventeen.

"My father had left enough money for us to live on, and there was carefully put aside also a sum that would give me a university education."

For this he went to Italy, determined to study architecture. But Boris, who is five years younger than I, was born in an age when the potentials of electricity were still being explored, when Marconi had invented the wireless, and, with many other young students, he was unable to resist the fascination of these new discoveries. He changed his university course from architecture to physics.

He went on holiday with four other Italian students, two girls and two boys, to the island of Ischia, just a few miles across the sea from Capri.

"We were very young, you know, Gracie, and full of lofty ideals. We made a pact that we would have a very platonic holiday, there would be no romance or anything like that you understand, we were much too 'intellectual' to fall in love."

Boris grinned at me. "I should have learned even then that one is never too studious to fall in love. We all *three* fell in love with two girls, and one of us was obviously odd-man-out, but we didn't know which one!

"So, I suggested that we three boys should draw lots as to which should be the 'loser,' and whichever of us was unlucky, he should say he had to go back to Rome to do some work, and not tell the girls why. I drew the odd-one-out, and I went. I felt very lonely.

"It was a lovely summer that year. When my boat reached Naples I thought of the long hot train journey up to Rome, and then I saw a boat marked 'Capri.' I'd always wanted to see this beautiful island; there was nothing nor anyone to stop me, so I got on that boat and went there for the day."

Boris climbed up the steep hill from the harbour to the Piazza, and stood looking out across the Bay of Naples. "One of those dramatic Mediterranean thunderstorms scudded into force. In a moment the blue sea became leaden and black, the sky heavy and sullen. It all reminded me of the Black Sea on whose shores I'd lived as a child. Somehow it made me feel at home.

"When the storm passed as suddenly as it began, it left the island all newly-washed and glistening. It was very beautiful. Although I was there quite by myself, suddenly I did not feel so alone. Instead, I felt as though I belonged to this island, that it would always be a place to which I could return, as though there'd be a welcome for me—yet I had not spoken a word to anyone. Can you understand?"

I could understand very well, for I had felt exactly the same way about Capri myself, and equally for no especial reason.

Then Boris went back to Rome. There he haunted the small shops which sold odd parts from which you could make your own wireless sets, and all the newest literature published on radio. At this time radio had begun a world-wide "do-it-yourself" vogue, and attracted the interest of men from all walks of life. The little shops specialising in radio parts became sort of small clubs where the fascinated customers discussed their latest progress and findings in making their own sets.

The lonely student who was Boris made friends with them. There was one who always talked with him, and later he discovered him to be Prince Colonna, a man whose family is one of the oldest in Rome, and who, himself, was a keen radio amateur.

From this chance acquaintance Boris met the Cerio family. He went to Capri again on holiday by himself and Prince Colonna was there also.

Already Boris had noticed that one house, in a beautiful and isolated part of the island—the same spot where I was to buy my house only three years later—had a very large wireless aerial.

"Tell me," he said eagerly to Prince Colonna, "do you know who has that splendid aerial?" The Prince told him it belonged to friends of his, the Cerio brothers, George and Edwin. They had brought over from America one of the first large radio sets ever to be produced; it was a sort of a museum piece, and very valuable.

Boris was fascinated and longed to see it, but there seemed no chance of that.

The Cerios were rich enough to make a hobby of keeping up with, and, if they could, getting ahead of all the newest inventions in the science of sound. The elder brother was a specialist in optics; the younger was a famous naval architect and engineer and a pioneer in submarine construction. They were not the sort of people to whom one could take a casual visitor easily.

Yet not much later Boris had the chance to meet them. The prized radio set broke down. Dr. George Cerio, the elder brother, thought he would have to take the whole thing back to America. Then Prince Colonna suggested Boris should have a look at it. "He's only a young student in Rome, but he's miles ahead of anyone I know in understanding these things," Colonna had said.

"The day I went to see Dr. Cerio was a great occasion for me," said Boris simply. "I was very nervous, and very impressed with his wonderful workroom and experimental laboratory; it was like a surgery, so beautifully precise.

"I knew Dr. Cerio was watching me, and I sensed that he liked the way in which I selected the tools for my work, only the few I felt necessary. I was so fascinated with the work, and so anxious to do it well, that I got to his house every morning as soon as it was light, and he gave me the key of the laboratory to let myself in. In eight days the set was working again, and my stock went high. That evening he was so pleased that he invited me into his home to have a Vermouth with him and his wife, and we talked a great deal. For me it was an evening of glow. I was very happy and proud.

"Then he gave me another radio set to re-model for him, and told me to come to his laboratory whenever I chose.

"I remember how privileged I felt. I respected Dr. Cerio's great education and learning. I felt honoured to be working for him. Every night I was so careful to replace all the tools I used exactly as I had found them.

"I was so afraid of trespassing on his privacy at all, or of doing anything which might spoil this wonderful privilege which had been given to me. Through the window of the workroom I could see his beautiful gardens, but I never dared to walk in them. And I was so afraid of being in his way that every day I would leave before noon and walk back

to the Piazza for my meals in case he felt he might have to
ask me to stay to lunch. I was so happy that I wanted to go
on for ever, just as I was. But I knew that Dr. Cerio was due
to leave soon for one of his long stays in America.

"I was thinking I must say good-bye to the beautiful
workshop, when, one morning, he knocked on the door,
and came in. He always knocked on the door, though it was
his laboratory—and I liked this so much in him.

"It was the day before he was leaving. He said: 'I realise
that I have never asked you what I owe you for your work,
and I know you are only a young student, but I did not
wish to embarrass you.' He left me an envelope which he
asked me to open later. Inside was a cheque for a thousand
lire which was a great deal of money in those days, and
meant very much to me.

"I began to tidy up the laboratory for the last time, when
Dr. Cerio came back again. This time he gave me another
envelope with two keys in it, one to the grounds of his
estate, and the other to his laboratory. 'Your holidays are
not over yet,' he said. 'Come here and work whenever you
want.'

"And then for a third time he came back, to say good-
bye. That's when he really decided for me what I would do
with my life.

"He said he felt that I had a flair for invention, and the
kind of mind that would have more scope for progress in
experiment than by remaining at a university, and he offered
me the chance to stay and work with him.

"I thought about it very much, Grace. By this time I
really belonged nowhere, nor to anyone. Both my sisters
had married, and if I had gone back to them I would again
have been the odd-one-out, something I have always hated.

"I loved Italy. I loved Capri especially, and to do experimental work of this sort, in radio and in sound, was the

dream of my life. What did it matter if I did not get my degree? I was responsible to no one. I had a little money left over from my unfinished university course, and I could always earn enough to keep myself, and my little room up in the square, by doing local radio repair work if it was necessary, for my requirements were very few. I agreed to stay."

That was in 1927 when Boris was twenty-four.

"Those years were wonderful for me," said Boris. "I became very close to Edwin Cerio, the younger brother, who did not leave Capri so frequently as George. For me it was a great privilege to share Edwin's mind, for he was a man of great learning. Under his mantle I met a lot of clever and interesting people. He gave me the entrée, which I should never otherwise have had, to meet all the élite who came to Capri.

"We built and made our own wire recording machine long before such things were put on the market. I remember when the Crown Princess of Italy was not well, she came to stay with the Cerios to rest, and we had much fun in recording her voice and playing it back to her.

"We built our own television receiver, again, long before they came on the market. As early as 1934 we got some of the B.B.C.'s first experimental pictures on our screens. We wrote to them and they were intrigued to think reception was possible so far away from London.

"And we saw one of their first transmissions, of a woman singing. Do you know who it was?"

I shook my head. "It was you!" said Boris delightedly.

So that was Boris's life for twelve years. He was absorbed in the Cerio laboratory; he filled his leisure hours roaming the beautiful island, reading every book he wanted to read, studying languages, meeting highly educated and cultured people. He never left Italy. And then the war came.

"I suppose, Grace, I never realised till then that, underneath all my contentment and tranquility, I was a lonely human being," he said.

Boris had to leave Capri, then a military zone, because he still held a Roumanian passport. He went to a little village near Vesuvius, some distance from Naples.

"I knew no one at all, and I was a foreigner, even though I *felt* Italian. I was not allowed to work because my radio work would have immediately caused suspicion that I was spying. Every day I had nothing to do and no one to talk with. I just had to walk, read, and sit in the small room which was all I could afford to rent."

I thought of the intolerable loneliness which must have engulfed Boris then. He had, in a way, escaped from the realities of life when he was still a young lad. And then the isolation of war suddenly forced him to realise that a lifetime spent in work and books and study builds you no human relationships at all, and that just when you need them most, you have none.

But Boris was smiling. "But after all, Grace," he said, "my work with my radio brought me everything, yes, even you! Wait, I will tell you.

"At first the loneliness, and the nothing to do, was bad. But then the police chief of the village—he wanted his radio mended—and someone said 'What about that Signor Boris?' So I obliged him, and he became friendly towards me.

"Then the Mayor, he wanted his radio looked at. The authorities in Naples had said I must not work with radio, but the Mayor was a very important man . . . and the police chief said 'Ask Signor Boris,' so I began to work again. This way I managed."

He managed till 1943 when the British reached Southern Italy. Boris wondered what would happen to him next.

"But my radio work still helped, you see. The British Army had to build airfields and their Airfield Construction Group needed an interpreter to act as a liaison officer between the Italian technicians and civil labour, and the Royal Engineers. As I knew a lot of technical terms involved in this sort of work in both English and Italian, I got the job."

So that was how Boris came to wear a sergeant's uniform and "join up" with the Eighth Army. He was with them for three years, and covered most of the Italian campaign with the advanced construction unit: that's how he learned to speak, and swear!—in English.

When peace came and the British troops gave him a fine send-off, he went back to Naples. There the N.A.A.F.I. headquarters was in trouble, and needed some skilled help with its Intercom system. Again someone said, "What about Boris, that fellow from the Royal Engineers?" Boris joined the N.A.A.F.I.

He got back to Capri in 1947, about six months after I returned there from my war travels, and went to live at the Cerio home, just 200 yards away from me. From the window of his room he looked across to my gardens and saw me many times.

Four years later we met.

And, at that first meeting when I was tearing round the place in my bathrobe trying to look after twenty-seven visitors, apparently I lived up to the impressions he'd always had of me. I can't say they were exactly flattering.

Boris had known of me as "that crazy English film star, Gracie Fields."

He'd seen, and *heard* me yelling and splashing about in the sea in front of my house, always with lots of people.

He had watched with horror when Monty and I had started blasting our rocky terraces to build our swimming pool. While the blasting went on it had churned the blue sea to a filthy yellow. Many people in Capri had tried to stop us building the pool, and Boris had actually taken a colour film of the sea, as evidence to use in a protest to the authorities that I was ruining the natural beauty of the island!

He'd been in the San Carlo Opera House in Naples when I'd sung "Land of Hope and Glory" there on Armistice Night and then, to his mind, desecrated the place by doing two broad comedy numbers as encores . . . in an Italian *Opera* House!

I found out that, at the beginning, I was not Boris's ideal woman by any means, and he'd come to mend my gramophone when I'd asked him, partly out of kindness for Monty's widow, and partly out of curiosity to see if this Gracie Fields was actually anything like the picture he'd formed of her. That first day it had seemed that I was.

"Now, perhaps, you see why it was I was so afraid that to fall in love with you would be disaster for me, because I did not think it could ever come true with you," Boris said quietly.

"I realised that my world was so small, living always alone, while you belonged to the whole world. What seemed to me everything, to you must have seemed nothing.

"But after our first few meetings I remembered every look on your face, every word that you said, and I tried to keep telling myself that you would not even be aware of my existence.

"When you came back from Canada and met me in the square, you said, 'It's so good to be back and see the faces I know' and I thought, 'Oh Hell! How many millions of faces she knows, and I'm only just one among them.' Yet I was tremendously grateful that you had recognised me at all.

"I tried very hard not to kiss you, you know. And afterwards I was sure you were offended. When you went to London again I tried to think that I had been lucky enough to know one fragment of pure happiness with someone, and that it would last me all my life. I didn't dare to dream that I might have it for always. . . .

"The day I asked you to tea and you didn't come because it rained, I thought: she's from the North, she could come over if she wanted to. She's a daughter of the North, she is used to the wind and the rain, the mild Capri Sirocco wouldn't stop her. She doesn't want to come."

"Oh, Boris," I said, "you know now how much I wanted to come. I was afraid you'd think I was chasing you!"

"And the evening we first went swimming," confessed Boris, smiling to himself. "I'm not a great diver you know, but I was like a child. When I dived off those rocks I thought 'I must make a good dive, do it well, otherwise she will despise me.' I was most afraid I would go in 'plop' and you would think I was just a stupid middle-aged man showing off! I was so grateful when I managed to dive fairly well.

"And then, when I took you to the little restaurants in Capri where you hadn't been before, I was afraid you would find them silly, and not smart enough after all the expensive places you were used to."

"They were just the sort of places I've always wanted to go to," I said.

"The loneliness in the war taught me there was so much in life I had missed," he said slowly. "I know now that all my learning I have had with my mind and with my imagination, from books. All your learning you have had with your heart and your spirit, and from experience; that is so much better. I felt very humble when I first dared to believe you had even noticed me."

"Well, you needn't, lad," I said. "I feel very ignorant when I realise how much more educated you are than I am, I feel positively stupid beside you sometimes."

"Well," said Boris cheerfully, "now we are married we will have time to share the learning we both know—what would you call it?—we can swop!"

And that's just what we have been doing ever since.

Boris made those things in my life which I had been taking a bit for granted, seem new and exciting to me. He had never been outside Italy since 1925, and because going to Canada, America, England, Europe . . . travelling in liners, flying in planes, was all for the first time for him, it became like the first time again for me too.

In many ways it *was* for the first time. Because of his eight languages, Boris is immediately at home in any country, and he wants to see that country in his own way, usually from the top of a bus. I've always longed to travel in this way, and never been able to do it. Always there was the best and the most central hotel, business managers, hired cars, smart restaurants, smart people, who always terrified me. Now I go riding on top of a bus with Boris in any country, and I love every minute of it.

Boris came with me to England for the first time in 1952 when I went to do a concert at the London Coliseum in aid of the Lynmouth Flood disaster.

That's when he met my mother and father who were still alive then.

"I was afraid they might have been cold and reserved and thought me a foreigner," he confessed to me afterwards, "but they were warm, and so nice. I thought you were exceptional, Gracie, but all your family match you."

And my mother, with her usual pithy comment, had taken one look at Boris and said: "Hmm, happen you've found the right one this time!"

On the night of the Coliseum concert Boris was with Bert and Lillian Aza in a box to the right of the stage. For the first time he was going to watch me working in a London theatre.

"Don't come with me to the dressing-room," I'd asked him. "Just go straight to your seat so that I know you'll be there when I come on."

I wanted to be alone in my dressing-room that night. Of all theatres I think I love the Coliseum most; it's big, warm, challenging, exciting, the very essence of music-hall which is where I really belong.

I had played in it ever since I first made a name for myself, and it holds many memories for me. That night, as I made up, many of those memories came back.

I saw myself again at the beginning of it all . . . when Sir Oswald Stoll had asked me if I could run across from the Alhambra Theatre to the Coliseum to do a ten-minute single act there—in between my "waits" in my first West End show, *Mr. Tower of London.*

The Coliseum was where I earned my first one hundred pounds. Those ten-minute acts had led to so much—to every other leading variety theatre in London.

I remembered the Royal Command performances and other shows, some that I'd done with all the family. The time when Mumma had sung with me from the stage, louder and better than I!

I remembered the recordings we'd made when Dad had joined in and insisted on doing his morning shaving song: "Hoh! You'll never miss your mother till she's laid beneath the clay!" And Mumma's furious nudge at him: "Shut 'oop, Fred, you mak' us sound so common!" Bless them both.

I thought of the time I'd sung on the London stage just before I was so ill, and the time when I came back there after the war—and the last time, only a year ago, when I'd sat in my dressing-room and been unable to think of anything or anyone except Boris.

Now Boris was out there, in front, and in a minute I'd face that wonderful audience again, knowing my husband was among them, and that after the curtain he'd be waiting for me, and we should go home together. "Our Gracie" and his Gracie too.

What matter that I'd dreamed of a night like this since I was seventeen, and I was now getting on for fifty-seven . . . now it was here.

I heard my call, my orchestra cue, and went on stage. Suddenly everything in life I'd ever wanted seemed all mine in that moment. I wanted to shout it, sing it, chuck it over the footlights at the audience in a great burst of happiness.

I felt as though a hundred champagne corks had popped inside my heart. I wanted to make the whole world laugh and be happy with me. My voice wasn't enough for once. In the middle of the show the whole bubbling loveliness that was life for me just bust, and I turned a cartwheel! I HAD to do something, and I think that Coliseum audience knew it.

That cartwheel was my way of saying, "Life's wonderful! At any age, at any time, no matter how long you have to wait: it's all worth it, for all of us, for you, me, everybody. LISTEN! It happens in the end . . . it all comes true!" And I turned another.

The way they laughed and cheered made me feel I'd got it over to them.

Boris was in the dressing-room waiting for me. The applause was still roaring out from the front. He just held out his arms. "Gracie, you are a very great artiste," he said simply, and there were tears in his eyes.

For once in my life I found the right words at the right

time. "It's not that," I said. "It's just that I'm a very happy and contented woman, and happiness is catching. Before, I've been able to conjure it up and pass it on; tonight I didn't even have to think about it or try. I didn't do anything. It was all there, and, tonight, that was because of you." And that was the plain truth.

Boris and I went up to Rochdale when the Queen and the Duke of Edinburgh were there on a Royal visit, and the town which has given me so much gave Boris something which helped him to understand, more than a million explanations from me, what it means to be called "Our Gracie." They called him "Our Boris!"

After the big concert in the Hippodrome he was sitting with the Mayor when the audience began to chant: "We want Boris! We want Boris!" And Boris had to go down on to the stage.

For me it was another of those times in which you suddenly see the whole of your life telescoped into one moment. This was the stage which my mother had scrubbed, where I had first sung as "Young Grace Stansfield, Rochdale's Own Girl Vocalist," and now, where my husband, born in a far-off land, shy, unused to crowds, was facing hundreds of Lancashire folk who had known me and my family all our lives.

Boris looked wonderingly at the huge audience, and then at the microphone before him. Suddenly he gave a wide smile and said: "Thank you, and please may I tell you this has been a wonderful privilege for me, to see my wife—your Gracie—presented to your lovely Queen. I shall always remember this day and keep it in my heart." And Rochdale cheered its own heart out to him.

We were staying with my Auntie Margaret, the one who was my dresser for so many years, the one who married the undertaker. She lives in Rochdale now.

Auntie Margaret has a portrait of me taken when I was young which I knew Boris would covet, and it's the only one in existence. Sure enough, Boris promptly noticed the portrait, and admired it to the point of asking Auntie Margaret if he could have it.

"Nay, ah'm not giving thee that!" she said firmly. "But ah've told Grace, ah'm leaving it to you in my will!"

Boris decided he couldn't wait that long, and asked if he might borrow it for a short time in order to have a copy photographed from it. He went out to get this done and to have a quiet look round Rochdale. He didn't know Rochdale! He was driven back in a car.

Everywhere he'd gone people had recognised him, stopped him, called him "luv," talked to him about "Our Gracie."

He'd been taken to see my grandmother's, Chip Sarah's, first shop; one of the houses where I'd lived; and finally, the little school where I'd gone as a "half-timer" when I was working in the mill. It was from the school that he'd been driven back, after promising he'd bring me straight back to the school with him to talk to the kids. The afternoon ended with Boris and me thumbing through the old registers to 1913 where, against my name was marked, time after time: "Absent. Sickness. Note from father."

"That's when I was off singing for my pork pies and my dad said he would never write another excuse note," I said, "and when you were buried in your books, like a good lad."

"Oh, I wasn't good," Boris protested quickly. "When I was young I hated to be mediocre to anything, I always wanted to be the best. But there was a boy at school who was a cripple and he was by far the best scholar, no one could beat *him*. When I found that he would *always* be the best I still couldn't bear to be only in the middle, so I decided I would be the worst! And I was!"

This passion of Boris's for "the best" led to our first quarrel.

Because he knows a great deal about microphones and recording he is what I would call a purist; every tone, every shading of a tone, must be exactly right. But he has always had time in life to wait for the ultimate in perfection. I haven't. I've always done my best, and then got on with the next thing.

So one day, when Boris was with me while I was working, he started to protest about all manner of things about the recording, including the type of microphone provided.

"It's not right for your voice," he stormed. "They should take more time . . ."

"Time costs money in this business, Boris, and it's perfectly all right."

"You don't know what you're talking about," said Boris angrily. "I do . . . and another thing, the orchestra, they are smoking while you're singing. *That's* not right for your voice. . . ."

"But I don't *mind*, and it doesn't make any difference. I wasn't brought up in a greenhouse. I'm not going to start being fussy now."

"You should start!" Oh, the argument went on and on, long after the (very successfull) recording was over.

I ended up in tears. Boris went off in stony silence.

I was the first to speak; I can't bear atmospheres. "I've made some tea, luv," I called to him. "Come on." He came, still quiet.

"I'm sorry . . ." I began.

"No," he said then. "I'm sorry, for my silence, I mean. Being alone for so long, I can keep silences. I know sometimes I have a bad temper, my sisters used to tell me that when I was young. Someone not so nice as you wouldn't have helped me out of it so quickly. But, even so, you shouldn't have got so upset."

"I think it's awful that we could quarrel," I said.

"Oh, no!" said Boris surprised. "You mustn't think that. Surely we shall quarrel some more?"

"No! Boris, No! I don't want to."

"But you'll *have* to," said Boris. "Two people, two thinking, sensible people don't live together every day of their lives *without* any quarrelling. If they do, then it means that one of them is continually giving in to the other, and that is very bad. They must argue, or quarrel things out, it's all a part of living.

"Sometimes you will find me very slow, or too thoughtful, or too cautious. Sometimes I know I will find you too impulsive, too reckless, too many jokes, like signing your cheques 'Sarah Siddons' or 'Fanny Adams' . . . you really mustn't! There will be days when I will want to be quiet and you will want to be noisy, but all this is natural. We learn about each other that way. Now, about your recording yesterday, you have a wonderful voice and you were using the *wrong* microphone. . . ." And I had to laugh.

But he was right. After that long talk Boris and I reached a compromise over recording sessions. I now use the mike he suggested and it *is* better. The boys still smoke while I sing. I like them to, and it doesn't bother me, so why should it bother Boris?

I told him how once, the great opera singer Tetrazzini came to see me when I was doing cod-opera dressed as a charwoman, but hitting the right top notes all the same.

She had asked me if I considered studying for operatic singing, for she thought I could. "No," I'd said, "it's not just the singing, it's the music-hall, the laughter, the people I work with, the people who come to hear me. It's the feeling that you do best where you belong that counts most, and I belong here." And I've always felt that way.

"So you're not making a prima donna out of me now, lad, whatever else you may do for me," I told him.

There are so many things since then that Boris has done for me, the hundred little things that go to make up a marriage. Perhaps one story can best tell them all. It was when we were in America a couple of years back. We'd just got to New York, and I was feeling terribly ill. I fell into bed and sent Boris out into a heavy snowstorm to buy me some castor oil, my mother's remedy for all ills!

Next morning it was obvious that I *was* very ill. Doctors came; by the afternoon I was in an ambulance on my way to hospital for an emergency operation for gall-stones.

With the single-mindedness that you can get when you are in great pain, all I wanted was that the operation should be done at once, anything to get me out of my misery. But Boris was nearly frantic.

Not until I came round did I realise all that he had done for me, nor, perhaps, quite how much I meant to him.

He had nearly driven the hospital staff barmy, and only with the greatest difficulty had they been able to keep him out of the operating theatre itself!

While I was unconscious he was quite alone in his anxiety in a strange city where he knew no one.

Suddenly he remembered the name of a Russian doctor who had once stayed in Capri, and was now working in New York. He made dozens of telephone calls till he tracked this man down. Then he demanded that he should come to hospital, and make sure that they were doing everything that was right and best for me, which the Russian doctor obligingly did!

Boris then went back and packed up all my belongings,

even to my jars of make-up and the magazines which had been by my bedside.

All these things he started to litter about my hospital room.

"What are you doing in here?" the nurses demanded.

"I'm putting all the same things about so that when Gracie wakes up, it will look the same and she won't feel lost," said Boris, setting out the austere hospital dressing-table like a boudoir.

"You can't do that!" said the outraged nurses.

"Oh, yes, I can!" said Boris, and stood his ground.

"Well, you must leave now because she'll be coming back from the operating theatre in a minute."

"And I shall be here," said Boris.

"No, Mr. Alperovici, you can't stay here."

"Oh, yes, I can," said Boris.

When I regained consciousness the first things I saw were my husband's smile, and all the familiar bric-à-brac of my own bedroom surrounding me.

Now I was all right the doctors assured him, and he must leave.

"What!" said Boris. "After all this time I have spent wondering if she would ever come back to me. Leave? Oh, no. I am staying with her in case she needs anything. It is my right, do you understand?"

They understood—and so did I.

And when we got back to the small flatlet which we had in New York he refused to think of letting anyone do anything for me except himself . . . even to the cooking, and to washing out my nylons. When we're on tour he's better at washing the "smalls" than I am to this day!

So there you are. I'm a very happy woman, and a very lucky one. I was lucky enough to receive two American television awards for my first straight play on T.V., J. M. Barrie's *The Old Lady Shows Her Medals.*

And, I might say, those awards gave me as much of a thrill as my first notices from the London Coliseum . . . well, never mind how many years ago! . . . the years don't count.

What does count? I think I know now.

Just recently Graham Greene, the author, asked me if I would go across to Naples to sing for some of the youngsters who come from the worst slums in the world there.

These boys are called the "Scugnizzi," meaning the "spinning-tops," for they have no place to eat, sleep or go to school, so they dart about stealing, and doing many worse things, to live; they sleep in the gutters.

Naples is a city of some two hundred thousand unemployed adults and fifty thousand homeless illiterate children who, because of the poverty and awfulness of their lives, are notoriously violent, cunning and untameable. Sailors, who always come across to see me when their ships dock in Naples, constantly complain about them: "Gracie, they hung on our arms, stole our wallets, snatched our cigarettes, pestered us. . . ."

The police could do little with them, there seemed no hope for them.

But a young priest, the now famous Father Borelli, dressed himself like one of the Scugnizzi, lived with them and behaved like them for months, to gain their confidence. And, from that small brave beginning, he has helped hundreds of them and organised some sort of a refuge for them. It is in a crumbling disused church in the heart of the poorest area of Naples. It was there I was asked to sing.

I was a bit nervous; I wondered how these tough youngsters would react to a middle-aged woman singer, and an

English one at that. Ah, well, perhaps they'd give me the biggest bird of my life.

I've sung in a good few places in my life but never in a ruined church with the plaster crumbling off its walls. "The House of the Urchins" they call it, and then the urchins came clattering in.

They eyed me, their faces expressionless. Some were noisy, others looked furtive.

Father Borelli, a pale, youngish man with a wide friendly grin and a broken nose, welcomed me.

What could I sing to a bunch of boys and youths hardened to a ruthless fight for existence before they were ten? Not love songs; not sad songs; gay ones then? We started off.

It took the first number to get them warmed up, a cheerful Neapolitan ditty which I sang in Italian with my good Lancashire accent, but they knew it.

Boris beamed encouragement; I beamed at the boys; they started grinning back.

We went into another song. More youths, ragged and unkempt, sneaked into the church. "Come on," I bawled at them. "You! Come on! Sing! *Canta!*" They got the idea. Soon we were all singing together. At the end of each song they clapped, shouted, stamped their feet for more.

When their applause got too loud I silenced them with my errand boy's whistle. It stunned even the Scugnizzi to silence.

Then, in my bad Italian, I talked to them a bit, told them I'd been a very poor little girl once too, I knew what it felt like to be poor, and cold, and, sometimes, hungry. I knew what it felt like to want things you couldn't have, and how you felt like taking them, when you didn't have any money.

"I've often felt like pinching things myself," I tried to

tell them. "We all do, if we're poor enough. I understand, Father Borelli understands, and that's why we all want to help you."

Somehow *they* seemed to understand. As I left those kids clustered round me, some of them shook my hand and the others shyly touched my arm or my dress.

Then Boris wrapped my coat around me and steered me through the cold, windswept alleys of the Naples winter to the warmth of our hotel.

As we walked along I felt in a curious mixed-up mood of exhilaration that was near to tears.

I was over sixty. I'd sung in the streets of Rochdale as a kid for pennies. I'd sung to Royalty, been honoured by them, and often treated like a queen myself.

There had been some bad moments and so many good ones—and what had I learned from it all . . . what counted most?

Some words that overworked, brave young Father Borelli had said, came back to my mind.

A few mornings later I'd just got our living-room ready for breakfast. In winter, in Capri, it's cold enough for a fire. I had a lovely log fire burning cheerfully in the grate; the little morning table was in the window alcove so that we could look out to sea while we ate. My favourite blue and white china looked nice against the white cloth, the toast was hot, the tea brewed.

I made the logs blaze up and called Boris to come for his breakfast. I thought, for the hundredth time, that this was one of my favourite times of each day now, a lovely beginning to every twenty-four hours, in my home which was now, at last, a *real* home.

"You know," I said to Boris as we sipped our tea, "I've got to the end of that story of mine, and I was trying to think, at the end of it all, what really does count most when you've lived a full life, and you try to add it all up.

"None of my family, and especially me, would be where we are today without my mumma. She was the driving force. Who's to say that I, and my sisters and brother, might not have been working in the cotton mills to this day if it hadn't been for her?

"She made all of us realise *her* ambitions for her, and all my life I've wondered, really, how she did it. She brought us up on clouts, and push, and never-give-in.

"Often we were down to our last ha'penny but it never made any difference to Mumma. So long as you didn't get soft and give in, you could always have a laugh the next minute, and a bit of a song, and you could always say your prayers at night and hope for something better.

"And I was thinking of that young Father Borelli the other night. I don't know if I've got his words exactly right, but when I told him how wonderful his work was, and how wonderful the faces of those boys had been when they sang he said: 'Signora Gracie, you see, with music, laughter, hard work—and the love of God, you can make everything come right in time.'

"You know, Boris, that's what it is, that's true. I think I've learned it now."

Boris smiled at me gently. "Gracie," he said quietly, "didn't you know? You learned all that in Rochdale, right at the very beginning."

INDEX

CPSIA information can be obtained
at www.ICGtesting.com
Printed in the USA
LVHW081515150121
676569LV00003B/4